# Contents

A Student's Guide to

# *Cabaret*

## directed by Bob Fosse

Richard McRoberts
B.A., M.Ed., M.A.C.E.
Marcia Pope
M.A., B.Ed., Grad.Dip. Children's Lit.

First published in 1999 by
Wizard Books Pty Ltd
ACN 054 644 361
P.O. Box 304 Ballarat 3353  Australia
Email: wizard@netconnect.com.au
www.wizardbooks.com.au

ISBN 1 876367 17 2

Cover design by Cressaid Media

Printed by Advance Press Perth

Wizard Books gratefully acknowledges the permission of Paul Brennan (Carrington Road Productions) to reuse the image of Liza Minnelli, from *Cabaret*, on the front cover.

# NOTES ON THE DIRECTOR
## AND SOURCES OF THE FILM

Bob Fosse (1927-1987) was probably the most famous dancer-choreographer of the American stage during the 1960s, 70s, 80s and early 90s. While Fred Astaire (much earlier) and Gene Kelly are better known for their film work, Fosse was regarded in recent times as the foremost 'song and dance man' on Broadway. His trademark modern, 'minimalist' numbers, with light costumes and a bare set (the typical wooden chair as prop dance) showed off the skills of the performers wonderfully. The constantly revived *Chicago* is thought of as the classic Bob Fosse show. He is also remembered for a small but dazzling range of musical films, which combined a background story with show-stopping stage numbers.

Born in Chicago to vaudeville parents, Fosse was dancing professionally at 14, acting not long after, and was a choreographer by 1954. His own dance style was soon noticed. He was incredibly athletic, turning cartwheels onstage, and capable of mesmerising acrobatics. As an actor he was unmemorable, but his dancing made up for it.

After working on the US stage for many years, he became involved in the filming of shows. He is best known for *Sweet Charity* (1969), *All That Jazz* (1979) – a semi-autobiographical study of a New York choreographer – and of course, *Cabaret* (1972). The dramatic sequences in these films were regarded by critics as competent, but it was the 'aggression and fire' of the musical sequences that really made them memorable. He also tried his hand at directing non-musical movies, notably *Lenny* (about the difficult career and life of the stage comedian Lenny Bruce).

*Cabaret* is regarded as his masterpiece. It combines a tortured love triangle, a striking recreation of pre-war Nazi Germany, and what one reviewer described as 'simply the snappiest, most devastating examples of fast and accurate timing [in dance] over a sustained period ever put on screen...a Fosse musical sequence remains an unmissable experience' (*The Illustrated Guide to Film Directors*, B&N, 1983). The film was a triumph for him. It went on to win

# NOTES ON THE DIRECTOR

Oscars for Liza Minnelli (Best Actress), Joel Grey (Best Supporting Actor), Bob Fosse (Direction), Geoffrey Unsworth (Cinematography), Rolf Zehetbauer, Jurgen Kiebach and Herbert Strabel (Art Direction), David Bretherton (Editing), Ralph Burns (Music Adaptation), as well as Knudson and Hildyard (Sound).

Bob Fosse received seven 'Tonys' for stage work and played Pal Joey twice on stage in 1961 and 1963. He married and divorced three times. He died of a heart attack just before the curtain went up for *Chicago* in September 1987.

C *abaret* started life long before Fosse's film. The characters and some vestiges of the storyline go all the way back to the 1939 short story collection, *Goodbye to Berlin*, by Christopher Isherwood (1906-1986). British-born Isherwood, the original of the Brian Roberts character in the film, came across from Cambridge in 1930, and lived for several years in Berlin, earning extra money as an English tutor.

In various stories, the inhabitants of Fraulein (Miss) Schroeder's boarding house (she becomes Fraulein Schneider in the movie) are described by Isherwood. Sally Bowles has her own story. The Sally of Isherwood's original is a somewhat scatty English girl who gets by on a small allowance from her disapproving parents, plus the money she makes by sleeping with wealthy men. She describes herself at one point as 'a little whore', and though Isherwood's Sally has a child-like vulnerability, there is little to admire about her. The Liza Minnelli embodiment of the character is infinitely more attractive. Isherwood's Sally does get pregnant, though not to Maximilian or Brian (there are no such characters in this version of the story), but to an egotistical film man called Klaus, who abandons her when his career takes him to England. Christopher Isherwood (the Brian character) assists her through the various crises of her life, puts up with her vainglorious dreams of success, and endures her exploitation of him, before she disappears out of his existence with just a brief note. Sally does (in the original) have ambitions as an actress, and wants to be in films. She does not, however, work in a club. The club referred to in Isherwood, though, which Sally and Chris (Brian) visit, 'The Troika', is very like the Kit Kat cabaret, with its telephones (very sophisticated in the early 30s), its *tableaux vivants* (nude acts) and its seedy atmosphere. There is no MC – an invention added for the Broadway show. Sally is comical, in a slightly pathetic way, a child-woman who believes her own fanciful dreams, and leads a rather amoral life.

The other originals of the story are there in different forms too. Christopher (Brian), the narrator, is the proper English gentleman, and Sally's friend. A wealthy American called Clive has the Maximilian role: he drunkenly spoils Sally and Chris (Brian) before vanishing and leaving them 300 marks. There is no hint of a *menage à trois* (triangle love affair) however. This, and the themes about corruption and materialism, were added for the movie. Fritz Wendel is the character we know from the film, but he does not seduce Natalia, let alone marry her, and he is not a Jew. Those complications were added later. Natalia is an eighteen-year-old, whom Christopher (Brian) befriends. It is her brother who is killed by the Nazis.

Isherwood's characters later inspired a 1951 dramatic play by John Van Druten, filmed in 1955 as *I Am a Camera*. This in turn produced the 1966 stage show *Cabaret*, produced by Broadway legend Hal Prince. It was perhaps only logical, given *Cabaret*'s success on Broadway, that it would eventually be turned into a movie. Fosse, who had worked on the show, was given the job of directing the movie, which came out in 1972. With its eight Oscar awards, *Cabaret* was a huge hit. Although it is now quite old, its radical themes (for the time), its brilliant musical numbers, and its unsettling storyline, have made it something of a cult classic. It was an early landmark film in the gay rights movement (see Themes section) and has been 'picked up' by the gay subculture as a film which accommodates sexual difference without disapproval. It allows multiple points of entry for gay audiences: identification with the dilemma of Brian, celebration of spectacle and engagement with the androgynous MC, as well as the accommodation of cross-dressing and what has been called the 'camp aesthetic' (ironic, playful and self-conscious adoption of costume and personae which break with the norms of the heterosexual world). However, its real audience is a much wider one, including all those who appreciate musicals of style and substance.

# THE TEXT IN PERSPECTIVE
## GENRE, STRUCTURE
## AND STYLE

*Cabaret* is of course a musical. Film theorists would call it an 'integrated musical' (where the song and dance are apparently 'natural' or integrated into the story, not 'time out' segments where the stars walk down city streets singing). Indeed, it forms part of the tradition of 'backstage musicals', in which we see the performers in dual roles – as performers on stage, and as 'real life' characters off the stage. *Like Singin' in the Rain* (1952) and other famous musicals, it offers dance, song and spectacle, but in a natural (ie. performance) setting.

It is not however a conventional musical, as the following observations argue. When we compare it to such old standards as *My Fair Lady* (1964) or *The Sound of Music* (1965), we see how radical it was (in its day), both in form and political subtext.

Firstly, it is a black comedy, or satire. From the opening scene, when the MC smiles wickedly straight into the camera, we know we are going to have our collective legs pulled. The club itself is peopled with individuals who are caricatures, from the fat businessman whom Sally is exploiting to the transvestite (in full drag) Brian meets in the men's toilet. The cabaret numbers are used as an ironic commentary on the 'real world' actions of the principal characters, or society itself. For instance, 'Money makes the world go round' is intercut with Sally's seduction by Maximilian, and 'If you could see her through my eyes', the grotesque parody love song in which the MC courts a gorilla in a dress, is bracketed alongside Fritz's love affair with the Jewish Natalia. The latter song, in case we had missed the reference to German anti-semitism (also brought out in the film) is underlined in the final words: '...she wouldn't look Jewish at all'.

Satiric musicals are a rare breed. Musical comedies are common, but singing films which sharply attack social vices are not generally considered 'good box office'. Three only come to mind: *Oh What a Lovely War* (1969), Richard Attenborough's very black singing commentary on the madness of war, *Little Shop of Horrors* (1986), a sci-fi spoof about a carnivorous plant that takes over the world, and *The Rocky Horror Picture Show* (1975), a high camp extravaganza sending up science fiction and movie melodramas, which has become a cult favourite. The former was a box office flop, though is still remembered fondly by anti-war activists, while the latter two are popular because the satire takes a back seat to full-on, over the top entertainment. *Cabaret* is one these unusual musicals that makes us laugh wryly, and think sadly about human nature at the same time.

Secondly, *Cabaret* is a film with a radical social or political message. Unlike such a film as *The Sound of Music*, which is underpinned by what we might term the utopian (everything is beautiful) Hollywood vision of family and (heterosexual) love and social cohesion, *Cabaret* engages with the notion of homosexuality (male in the foreground, lesbianism in the background), bisexuality, transvestism, abortion, promiscuity, and other traditionally taboo subjects (by Hollywood standards), treating them with respect and serious attention. It is important to remember that the movie was released in 1972, when the voice of second wave (modern) feminism was just emerging, and gay activism was practically unheard of. Most important of all, it rejects the customary 'happy ending', where the hero and heroine go off into the sunset (metaphorically speaking) arm in arm. *Cabaret* takes a much more cynical view of the world, exposing its principal characters in all their human imperfections (Sally's self-delusion, Brian's sexual confusion), rather than setting them up as models of mainstream conformist 'goodness'. It argues that people do routinely prostitute themselves for money or advancement, betray one another, and lead lives of perplexed meaninglessness – ideas that a traditional Hollywood 'feelgood' movie (and especially a musical) abhors.

The anti-Nazi message of the film fits in here, though it is hardly radical (after all, *The Sound of Music* is anti-Nazi). More importantly, and subtly, *Cabaret* offers the subversive hint that corruption is not a diabolical alien force coming from 'out there' (the bad guys, the foreigners), but is inside us, and linked to such everyday urges as sex and patriotism. The most unsettling scene in the film is probably the beer garden one (55), in which one by one the ordinary folk (not the seedy characters in the nightclub) are seen to be swept up in German aggression (the song 'Tomorrow' being about world conquest). This is reflected all along in the Kit Kat sequences with their low key hint of inward depravity under a glitzy, sweet-seeming exterior. *Cabaret* amuses, but it also makes some bleak comments about human nature, of the sort rarely seen in movies pitched at mainstream 'family viewing'.

It is reasonable to talk about *Cabaret* as a love story, though we must note how complex and unusual a 'romance' narrative it is. The Fritz-Natalia narrative is played quite straight, complete with happy ending. The film contents itself with showing us the admirable moment when Fritz 'outs' himself as a Jew, and marries the girl he loves. It does not (perhaps fortunately), attempt to depict what might have happened to two Jews in Germany a few years later, when Hitler's 'final solution' got seriously under way. The Brian-Sally narrative is rather more involved, and here again we see the film's 'downbeat', cynical bent. Brian, who (we deduce) thinks of himself as homosexual, discovers a capacity to love a woman. For a time, like other gay men before and since, he thinks he has gone 'straight', but the affair with the predatory Maximilian shatters that illusion. It does not, fortunately, shatter the bond with Sally. Brian tries, out of compassion and as part of an attempt to do 'the right thing' – but against his real instincts – to remain 'hetero' by marrying Sally and adopting the baby, but the pretence is detected by Sally, whose abortion ends the need for a charade. Sally's own misgivings about the domestic idyll she has fantasised also end with the abortion. At the conclusion of the film, we assume that Brian is reconciled to his bisexuality, and is going on to a life (away from Sally) which will involve liaisons of both kinds. There is a quality of quiet acceptance, and enduring fondness, between them in their final scene (58).

S tructurally, the film is built on a clever binary scheme, with the cabaret providing a 'theatrical space' in which themes are expressed in an entertaining manner (the songs' powerful subtext rendered palatable by the symbolic or caricatured way they are presented). An example is the obvious racial prejudice theme of 'If you could see her through my eyes'. It is not however 'rubbed into' us. The song is funny, and only turns nasty in the last line.

Similar themes are also enunciated in the 'realistic space' outside the club (the boarding house, the streets of Berlin, etc), but here they are enmeshed in all their real life complexity. For instance, we see Sally 'falling for' Maximilian. A variety of interpretations of this development are open to us, from the romantic to the cynical, but the cue is provided when the MC mouths the word 'money' (right in the middle of the dinner party, in a blatant, attention-grabbing 'cross cut'). The very explicitness of the 'moral' here, unthinkable in the realistic world of Sally, Max and Brian, is quite acceptable in the mouth of the MC, who inhabits an artificial world where anything can be said.

There is, not surprisingly in such a schema, considerable symbolism at work. After a while we sense that the club is a metaphor for Germany and the times: the grotesques are taking over, decadence is rampant, nothing is quite what it seems. The MC's mocking words, 'Here, everyone is beautiful', take on a sickly ring. We later see the beautiful Aryan boy singing the charming song 'Tomorrow'. It takes some time before we realise that his (and the song's) surface prettiness hides a dark inner nastiness (he is a Hitler Youth, and the song is about German conquest).

Stylistically, there is a complete contrast between the two 'spaces'. The cabaret sequences are lit with all the theatrical artificiality and cinematic flair the director can muster. We have dramatic high key (very bright) and low key (sombre) lighting, silhouettes, low angle shots, grotesque close ups, sweeping camera movements, fast edits, rhythmic effects and shock convention-breaking moments (as when the MC looks straight into the camera lens).

In contrast, the 'outside world' sequences are shot with carefully disciplined 'realism' – conventional medium shots and long shots for the most part, 'normal' lighting, no odd angles, a subdued editing rhythm. This difference is important. The two are meant to remain in a state of tension, one commenting on the other. Confusing the styles would have weakened the film, and undercut the powerful 'Greek Chorus' effect of the cabaret numbers and the MC. In Greek tragedy, the chorus functioned to comment on the action, making moral points. In *Cabaret*, the commentary (through the MC and musical numbers) is primarily ironic and subversive.

# READING A FILM AS TEXT

Although film study requires discussion of techniques (plot, characterisation, dialogue, metaphor, etc) which are familiar from literature, it also works in its own ways, and needs its own vocabulary. Below, with illustrative examples from *Cabaret*, is a reminder of specifically filmic techniques which need attention. Further examples appear in the commentaries which follow.

## Actors and Acting

Performers bring the story to life in ways which colour our response. We are used to the convention that the actors *are* the characters; we suspend our disbelief, forgetting that they are players on a set, and feel for them as the 'real' people they are playing.

Liza Minnelli is a classic example of a performer who defines the part in a highly personal way. Minnelli, already a famous singer and dancer when she made this film, brought to the character of Sally her complex, seductive talents: her little girl, *ingenue* charm, her beguiling eyes, her wonderful throaty voice, and that suggestion of vulnerability or fragility which stops us from condemning her, no matter what she does. In the hands of a less skilled performer, Sally would have been tiresome and possibly squalid. Instead, Minnelli makes Sally the eternal 'little girl lost', and our hearts go out to her.

The same canny casting is evident in the choice of Michael York for the role of Brian. The good looking Englishman is every bit the proper gentleman, all politeness and emotional repression. His highly understated performance captures a tentative persona, and a sense of vulnerability. The low-key performance and absence of flamboyance provide a useful dramatic foil to Minnelli's vibrance.

## Mise en Scène

This is a French expression traditionally used in film analysis. It means 'scene setting', and refers to the design elements of the film, which, like everything else, are coded with meanings.

# Sets and locations

Cabaret is a striking example of the way one particular set comes to define a whole film. The Kit Kat Klub, dominated by the brightly lit stage, is at once mesmerising and disturbing. From the very first shot, with its reflective but distorting mirror surface, through a variety of acts, garish, vulgar and occasionally poignant, to the final shot (also in the mirror), we are invited to read the cabaret as a metaphor for what the whole film is about. It is on the surface playful, carnival-like, but underneath a caricatured version of real life, with elements of the grotesque and the decadent. Nothing is quite what it seems. Reality can be manipulated. People can be played upon. In the cabaret, this hardly matters. In real life, it is more than a little dangerous.

Other locations are equally eloquent. Consider the impression created by Maximilian's country estate. Its unthinkable opulence establishes by itself the seductive appeal of money and privilege. In contrast, the streets of Berlin glimpsed in several scenes establish economically an atmosphere of grinding ordinariness, and elements of paranoia and violence.

# Clothing, make-up and accessories

Most striking perhaps are the stage costumes worn by the cabaret performers. The 'orchestra', for example, a group of women in flimsy costumes, with suspender belts and high heels, set the tone of decadence almost single-handedly. This air of seediness is reinforced in the provocative clothing worn by the dancers, and of course accentuated by their 'come hither' antics.

Although she exists in a class of her own, Liza Minnelli's Sally has a range of stage costumes which evoke the idea of 'decadence': the famous little black number ('A fine affair'), and the 'flapper' costume ('Money'). Offstage, her costumes are equally flamboyant, and are symbolic of her vivacity and narcissism. These qualities are most evident if we contrast her dress style with Natalia's.

The Germanic folk costumes of the dance number (Scene 11) and 'Two Ladies' are used in conjunction with a caricatured dance style and extreme camera angles to foreground the theme 'Nothing is what it seems' (and to advance the film's critique of Germanic nationalism and its connection to Nazism). The grotesque gorilla suit of 'If you could see her through my eyes' is an even more pointed device (showing via costume what racism means). Although in formal dress suit, the MC's makeup and hairstyle undercut any impression that he represents respectibility. The visual mismatch establishes a disturbing, if not diabolical, persona.

The costumes worn by the characters off stage establish the era, the class, and the personalities of the different individuals. Consider Fritz's threadbare gentility, Brian's genteel English clothes, Maximilian's stylish clothes. Worth noting as a special case are the brown shirts, and the swastika armbands, which appear with alarming frequency as the story progresses, that latter a symbol so powerful that Fosse is able to end the whole film on it, knowing what devasting meaning the audience will read into it.

# Lighting and Colour

As with other aspects of the film, there is a sharp contrast between the way these visual markers are set up for the cabaret sequences, and for the 'real life' sequences.

In the Kit Kat, the stage is brightly lit, colorful, even garish. By contrast, the clients of the club are often seen in a murky gloom, consistent with the theme of decadence. The cabaret is a place of performance.

In the world outside, although there are still some highly theatrical scenes (the picnic sequence, the boat scene, and the beer garden), most settings are shot to create the impression of 'normality'.

# Camera Angles

Placement of the camera is a vital signifier of meaning. Shooting a player from below is conventionally used to make him/her seem impressive and admirable; from above can make him/her look powerless. In this film, however, irony often complicates such a pattern. For instance, the MC, shot repeatedly from a low angle, is portrayed as controller of the cabaret, but, in conjunction with his makeup and facial expressions (see above), the camera angle makes out a case for him being frightening and dangerous, rather than admirable.

Extreme camera angles can also help focus on the nature of events. For example, the high angle shots of the sign 'Juden' painted on Natalia's steps, and of the dead dog, contribute to our growing sense of concern for the victims of Nazism.

# Framing

We are used to the terms 'long shot' (showing the whole scene at once), 'medium shot' (showing two or more people in reasonable detail) and 'close up shot' (showing usually one or two faces or other detail).

Extreme close ups are usually frequently in *Cabaret*. For instance, Sally's eyes often dominate the shot, capturing both her vulnerability and love of performance. The grotesque face of the MC is often accentuated by close ups. An striking instance of a close up which communicates complex psychological meaning is the one at the end of Scene 36 , when the three main characters dance slowly, face to face. The shot says it all. Its claustrophobic and sexually ambiguous depiction of the *menage à trois* is overpowering. Brian breaks from the group, unable to cope with his conflicting impulses.

# Editing

Editing in *Cabaret* is vital to both the argument of the film and the creation of atmosphere. Through the use of cross-cutting (linking shots from completely different scenes or places), the film makes ironic comment on events and characters. The classic example (Scene 34) is a cut from Maximilian's dinner party to a single brief shot of the MC mouthing the word 'Money'. Another clear instance is the way Scene 11 (the Germanic folk dance) is intercut with Scene 12 (the brutal beating of the nightclub owner).

The atmosphere of the Kit Kat Klub is economically established through a combination of shots of selected individuals (eg. the 'butch' woman) and wide shots of the whole space.

Editing allows the film to tell a number of stories simultaneously, and to make connections between the different narratives. For example, the conventional romance of Fritz and Natalia is contrasted with the complex and unconventional relationship of Brian, Sally and ultimately Maximilian.

## Sound

All films use the sound track (dialogue, music, sound effects, silence) to enhance meaning. While the song and dance acts of the cabaret are played for their entertainment value, they have a secondary function as well. Each carries some sort of symbolic meaning. For instance, Sally's rendition of 'Maybe this time' can be read as the star just singing a charming love song. It can also be seen as a comment on Sally's real life yearning for emotional fulfilment. The song 'Money', however, while appearing to argue for unfettered materialism, is ironic. Given the exaggeration and self-mockery built into the performance, it in fact makes out a case that money lust is tacky, if not decadent. The same ironic effect can be seen in 'Tomorrow belongs to me'. The superficial attractiveness of the song is belied by its lyrics, which embrace German expansionism (and by implication, the whole Nazi phenomenon).

# BACKGROUND NOTES

## ON THE NAZIS

Anti-Semitism (anti-Jewish prejudice) has a long and sordid history, going right back to the beginning of Christianity. The destruction of Jerusalem by the Romans in 70AD led to what is called the Diaspora (dispersal), as Jews, deprived of a homeland, scattered throughout the known world. In many countries, they were greeted with hostility. They usually lived and worked together, wore distinctive clothing and often spoke their own language. Furthermore, their supposed implication in the death of Jesus Christ was taken as justification for discrimination and violence. Especially in those countries where large Jewish minorities lived (Germany, Poland and Russia in particular), regular outbursts of anti-Jewish hatred flared up over the centuries. In many places, Jews were forced to live in segregated enclaves of cities (ghettoes) and even to wear identifying badges. They were often not permitted to own property or to hold political office.

Germany, after the First World War, was in a disastrous state. It had not only lost millions of men in the war, but had been forced into crippling compensation payments. Worst of all, it suffered the shame of losing. As if that wasn't enough, the Great Depression hit in 1929, causing massive unemployment, rampant inflation and economic breakdown in many sectors of the economy. People sought a scapegoat for all this chaos, and they didn't look far.

A young Austrian named Adolf Hitler, who had served in the trenches, was particularly bitter about the war, and blamed what he saw as an international conspiracy of Jews. When he was locked up in jail for participating in a rebellion in 1923, he wrote a book called *Mein Kampf* (My Struggle), in which he set out his theories about the racial superiority of the Aryan (white, blue-eyed, blond, European) peoples, and need to exterminate those of lesser races, such as the Semites (Jews). His racist theories and personal charisma spawned a political movement, and eventually a party, the National Socialist (shortened in German to 'Nazi') party. His supporters took to wearing brown paramilitary uniforms as a sign that they believed in his 'patriotic' theories. These are the 'brown shirts' we see in the film. For several years, as his party gained strength, his supporters contented themselves with massive rallies, and when drunk, privately beat up Jews and smashed the windows of their shops. The Nazi party systematically pumped out propaganda about Jewish crimes, and it was widely believed in the German community. The Nazis were considered hot-headed extremists, but at heart good Germans, and many saw their equally intense hatred of the communists as a way of keeping Germany free of the Stalinist peril.

In 1933, Hitler's party was voted into power and he became the new Chancellor of Germany. Shortly after, the Reichstag (Parliament) burned down, and the communists were blamed. Using this as an excuse, Hitler ended democratic rule in the country. His secret police, the State Police (Gestapo for short), tracked down its enemies and began to eliminate them. Later, his Schutzstaffel (SS) guard began setting up slave labour camps, to which political prisoners and other 'undesirables' were deported. Hitler also continued his aggressive expansionism, taking over neighbouring countries (the German-speaking part of Czechoslovakia, and Austria) by force, claiming they were German by right. This policy is referred to in the song 'Tomorrow belongs to me'.

In 1939, when he invaded Poland, war was declared. Germany invaded the Netherlands, Belgium and France, and German planes began to attack Britain. For a time it looked like Hitler was unstoppable. Meanwhile, he instigated the rest of his racist policy. Commissioning what was euphemistically called the *Endlosung* (final solution), he had Jews around occupied Europe rounded up, forced into ghettoes, then deported to *arbeitslagen* ('labour camps'). Secretly, several of these became death camps. At Dachau, Buchenwald, Auschwitz and other camps, Hitler's subordinates built gas chambers and began systematically murdering the enemies of the state. The extermination program got seriously under way in 1940, and soon up to 10,000 people a day were being killed.

The war dragged on. Hitler's early supremacy crumbled, and the allies counter-attacked, in the air, and later with land assaults. But it was not until April 1945 that allied troops took Berlin, and Hitler committed suicide. On May 8, the war ended. The sight that greeted the soldiers who liberated the camps was a terrible one. Those remaining were skeletal and traumatised. Those who had died numbered over 5,860,000. Most of the Jewish population of Germany, Austria, Poland, the Netherlands, Belgium, France, and other countries under Nazi influence had perished. This massive crime is now known as 'the Holocaust', which means total extermination.

The only good that can be said of this appalling period is that it led to the foundation of the modern state of Israel (1948), and to a permanent shift in people's consciousness about the evils of racism. Although the film *Cabaret* does not at all directly refer to the Holocaust, it is implicit in every single scene that has to do with the Nazis and their Jewish victims.

# SUMMARY

## COMMENTARY

### Scene 1: Title sequence

The screen is completely black. The titles, in a stark modern white font, appear against this backdrop. There is no sound whatsoever.

After the titles and the names of the leading players, sound is faintly heard in the background. At the same time, the blackness of the screen resolves itself into a dappled pattern. While we watch, it becomes obvious that the shapes we can make out are reflections in some sort of distorting mirror. Just before the titles end, we read, 'Berlin, 1931'.

### Scene 2: The Kit Kat Klub, interior, night ('Willkommen, Bienvenue, Welcome' )

A face appears in the mirror, grotesquely distorted. At that very moment, the camera pulls back to reveal the face of the Master of Ceremonies (Joel Grey). He turns and looks directly into the camera for a moment, leering. His face is made up in white, with contrasting red lips, and mascara. He is dressed in a tuxedo, and carrying a cane. He sings the opening song, 'Willkommen, Bienvenue, Welcome' (Welcome, Welcome, Welcome). As he sings and prances around the stage, we see that the setting is a nightclub. The lighting, the stage (visible at various camera angles) and the audience, seen both from behind and in 'cutaway' shots, all establish the setting. The song is bright and cheeky, the MC telling the audience to leave their troubles outside and enjoy the happy atmosphere of the club. 'Here, everyone is beautiful – the girls are beautiful – even the orchestra is beautiful.' He introduces his co-performers – the orchestra, an all woman ensemble, the dancers, and the other 'acts'. While the MC is singing the opening song, we cut away several times to:

### Scene 3: Berlin station, day

Several times we find ourselves watching a well dressed, innocent and eager looking young man (Brian – Michael York). The train arrives in the station. He looks out the carriage window. He descends from the train, and makes his way between the very ordinary looking German people on the platform. Later he is seen catching a bus and getting off at his destination. Each time we return to the cabaret, where the MC and performers are involved in presenting their set piece to the appreciative audience.

# Commentary

*Cabaret* is based, as the title suggests, on a cabaret stage show. This show is always nothing less than entertaining. The opening number, with its enjoyable Germanic folk song 'oom pa pa' rhythm, its bright lights, its colourful characters, and its naughty humour – is a good example. The tone is one of fun and cheeky merriment.

Although the other scene intercut with the opening song – the arrival of Brian – appears totally dissimilar, an arbitrary addition as it were, we will later remember the contrast. Brian is the archetypal innocent abroad – the fresh faced, 'squeaky clean' young man, coming to a foreign country for the first time, his face aglow with innocent expectation. The daylight scenes on the station and in the streets of Berlin, with its background characters all plain and earnest and ordinary looking, suggest normality.

In contrast, we begin to see that there is a dark undercurrent to the scene in the cabaret. The MC, a puckish figure, seems gleeful in an almost manic way. His androgynous (both male and female) or hermaphroditic face is vaguely disturbing. The mascara, bright red lips and white face make-up are both widely theatrical and slightly unsettling. The dancers, scantily clad in garish costumes, wiggling their hips and spreading their legs suggestively, contribute to a sense that the act, and perhaps the whole world it represents, is somehow, 'on the edge'. There are fragments of grotesquery – the 'butch' woman glimpsed early in the piece watching the show, the singer putting a shocking blond wig on, the fact that the orchestra too is dressed in sexy attire – all contribute to the sense of 'decadence'. This opening scene, which so cleverly sets the tone for the whole film, establishes a sense of the nightclub as some sort of uneasy metaphor – all show, cheap glamour and apparent fun disguising darker realities.

### Scene 4: Frau Schneider's boarding house, day

Brian arrives at the boarding house. He knocks at the door, which is opened by Sally Bowles (Liza Minnelli). He asks, in German, if there is a room to let. Sally asks him for a cigarette, and lets him in. When he notices her green fingernails, she comments on them, using the phrase 'divine decadence'.

She shows him through the boarding house, talking about its eccentric inhabitants, and showing him the small room that is available. He tells her he needs space to give English lessons, in order to pay the rent. She offers him use of her room when she is not there. She makes him a 'Prairie oyster' (egg and worcestershire sauce), puts on a record of lively dance music, and persuades him to stay. They chink glasses and drink. Brian is amazed at the taste. Sally laughingly tells him he has been given the toothpaste glass.

# Commentary

This scene, which introduces us to the two central characters, establishes a number of things about them personally. The most obvious is the amusing contrast between Brian's English reserve and Sally's American forthrightness. He is conservative, shy and 'innocent'. She flaunts her radical, free thinking lifestyle – the 'decadent' fingernails, the wholehearted embrace of the alternative culture in which she finds herself – not just the foreign milieu of 1930s Berlin, but the gay world already subtly referred to (the lesbian masseuse and the other vaguely radical inhabitants of the boarding house). She practically seduces Brian, and they have only just met. What does this signify? Is she outgoing and exhuberant, or a little desperate? How will Brian react to the immersion in this 'decadent' new world? We wait to see.

### Scene 5: The Kit Kat Klub, night ('A Fine Affair')

Sally is putting the final touches to her make-up in her dressing room, as the MC goes into his routine introduction of her song (which she knows off by heart). She comes on stage and goes into the musical number 'A Fine Affair'. It is a song about leaving a series of lovers, and repeatedly saying goodbye to 'Mein liebe Herr' (My Dear Sir). Sally and the scantily clad chorus girls, all draped suggestively over wooden chairs, go through the song, to the great enjoyment of the audience.

# Commentary

'A Fine Affair' is a classic Bob Fosse set piece. One of his signatures as a choreographer was this sort of number, with scantily clad women and the use of minimal stage props such as wooden chairs. The song is presented ostensively for its pure musical and theatrical appeal – cleverly choreographed, with slick use of lighting and enormous energy in the presentation. We are meant to enjoy the number for its own sake, seeing it as a vehicle for Liza Minnelli's and Bob Fosse's talents.

At the level of subtext however, once again, is the hint of something wrong. The lyrics of the song, about leaving a man with whom Sally (or the character) has had an affair, the suggestion of promiscuous 'bedhopping', is also part of what, on reflection, we take from the song. Once again, the idea of decadence, of amorality, comes out.

### Scene 6: The Kit Kat Klub, night, later

After the song, Sally changes and makes her way to the tables in the nightclub. She introduces Brian to her young friend Fritz Wendel, who pretends to be a businessman, but, as he admits to Brian when Sally goes off to entertain a fat businessman, he is really looking for a wealthy wife.

As Fritz and Brian are talking, the MC introduces the next act. It is mud wrestling, with two buxom women in revealing costumes. The wrestling takes place in a makeshift ring on the stage. The MC gleefully introduces the wrestling, and when they have started, sprays

them with water from a soda syphon. The audience laughs uproariously.

Fritz has been complaining about the economic times, as well
as the Communists and the Nazis. As this moment we see a 'brown
shirt' (one of Hitler's paramilitary supporters) in the distance. The
nightclub owner sees him and ejects him from the club.

Brian, who has been watching this, goes to the men's toilet.
He is standing at the urinal when he is joined by a woman. It turns
out to be a man in drag. Brian is amazed.

# Commentary

The theme of decadence, which has emerged subtly in both the
boarding house and 'A Fine Affair' scene, now becomes more
obvious. We have been introduced to Fritz, and reading between the
lines, begin to understand that he makes his money out of going with
wealthy women. He is in short a gigolo. Sally meanwhile is in the
business not only of singing but also 'entertaining' wealthy men.
Sally's facade of stylish radicalism now looks a little more suspect.

Picking up a similar idea is the mud wrestling episode. While
the musical acts are stylish and attractive, this scene is far more
debased. The leering of the MC, the extreme camera angles used, the
fast editing, and the close up shots of the audience, drunken and
animal-like in its response, is heavily satiric (mocking these people
and their lack of dignity) rather than celebratory.

The scene culminates when Brian is in the toilet, a moment
both comic and disturbing. The transvestite who stands next to him
at the urinal personifies the bizarre 'underworld' in which Brian finds
himself.

### Scene 7: Berlin street, night

Sally is asking Brian if he is surprised that she works in such an
'extraordinary' place. She asks him to tell her about himself, but
almost immediately interrupts him by telling Brian she wants to be a
great movie actress.

# SUMMARY AND COMMENTARY

## Scene 8: Berlin street, day

Brian mentions that he has been told by Fritz that Sally's father is an ambassador. 'Almost an ambassador', she corrects, telling Brian that her father visits her constantly, and takes her off for vacations all over. Sally suddenly asks Brian if he has ever slept with a girl. He answers that it didn't work out.

## Scene 9: Beer garden, night

Brian and Sally have been drinking. Sally reasserts that she wants to be an actress and, as they leave the beer garden, tells Brian about the openings she is almost getting and hopes to get. She hears a train coming and tells Brian to come with her.

## Scene 10: Berlin street, night

Sally pulls Brian along the street until they come to the point just below where a train is travelling on an elevated railway overhead. She leans against the wall and, her voice drowned out by the train above, screams without inhibition. Afterwards she pants with satisfaction. Brian asks what she is doing and she tells him it makes her feel good. She invites him to try it. He refuses, but when she teases him about his British reserve, he agrees. A train comes rattling along and Brian prepares to open his mouth.

## Scene 11: The Kit Kat Klub, night

The MC and chorus girls, dressed in traditional German folk dress (lederhosen, or leather pants with braces and long socks, with felt hats) are singing a lively German dance song, slapping one another in a jerky movement as they go. This scene is intercut with:

## Scene 12: The Kit Kat Klub, exterior, night

Four Nazi brown shirts are brutally beating the nightclub owner (who had earlier ejected one of them). We cut back and forth constantly between the dancing song in the cabaret and the beating. The rhythm of the two is almost the same. When the brown shirts have finished, the nightclub owner lies on the cobblestones, bleeding and immobile. The final open mouthed gesture of the MC at the end of the song visually mimics the open mouthed position of the dead nightclub owner.

# Commentary

All is not as it seems. The illusion of happiness and security fostered by the nightclub is undercut by what we see. Sally pretends that all is well with her globe-trotting father, but the implication is that she is lying, covering up for his indifference. Sally's ambitions (to become a great film star) look like being just pipedreams, while she leads in real life a tacky existence as a singer in a seedy club and perhaps selling herself on the side for money. There is a hint of Brian's as yet unrevealed sexual orientation in his cryptic remark to Sally about his lack of success with girls.

Meanwhile, the Nazi theme has become very powerful indeed. The posters in both the scenes where Brian and Sally are walking along the streets (Scenes 7 and 8) feature posters on the walls behind. Most of these posters, which are of Communist party officials, have been daubed in red paint and ripped. We have seen several Nazi flags. All this comes to a head in the brutal beating scene. In what is a painfully ironic 'counterpoint' (two elements playing off one another), we see a parallelism between the German folk song and the fatal beating administered by Hitler's supporters. The similarity of the rhythm and actions of the folk dancers and the Nazi beating suggests a connection. The editing encourages the viewer to see the link between the two (both being expressions of German nationalism and a society which condones violence and hate).

Even the bizarre screaming scene (10), apparently harmless and comic, is vaguely disturbing. Sally sees her behaviour as amusingly eccentric and liberated. In fact it suggests desperation and even mental instability. There is a hint too that this much 'letting go' may not necessarily be a good thing. As in the mud wrestling episode, and the beating, letting go, giving way to baser instincts, may be a sign not so much of liberation, as of uncontrolled animalism.

### Scene 13: Boarding house, day

Sally introduces Brian to a publisher, Herr Ludwig, saying she has arranged for Brian to translate a book into English. She secures an advance for him. Ludwig gives Brian the book, and the advance, and Brian agrees to do the translation.

### Scene 14: Boarding house, day

Sally is trying on various clothes. She finally selects a skimpy negligee. She enters Brian's room. He tells her that the book that he has agreed to translate is pornography, entitled *Cleo the Whip Lady*. Sally tells him that all Ludwig's works are 'dirty books'.

Simulating being cold (after the bath she has taken), Sally asks Brian to warm her. He does so, in an uncommitted manner. She kisses him, but he does not respond. Sally goes to her room, returns with a gramophone, and puts on a sensuous dance song. She sways suggestively. Frustrated and bewildered, Sally asks him if he sleeps with girls. He tells her he has gone through the motions three times, but that all were disasters. Sally finally understands. They agree to be friends, because as Sally says, friends are harder to find than lovers, and 'sex screws up a relationship'.

# Commentary

The truth is out at last about Brian. What were hints and reading between the lines, is now made explicit. Brian is homosexual. Sally has found out the hard way. What is most notable about this awkward, if faintly comic scene, however, is that the two have managed to negotiate a potentially explosive situation with dignity and kindliness. Brian's gentle rejection speaks well of him, and indeed this is a scene which endears Sally to us too. She has tried to play the *femme fatale* (seductress), but it is a clumsy attempt, and free of the predatory component. It says a lot about both her foolishness and her sweetness of disposition that she accepts Brian's rebuff so well. As in so many other scenes, she is redeemed by her child-like innocence.

## Scene 15: Boarding house, day

Brian is giving Fritz English lessons. Fritz tells him that he is looking for another opening, and admits that he is a gigolo. Brian tells him he is expecting a new pupil, a Miss Landauer. Fritz pays attention. The Landauers are rich Jews. He asks Brian if the pupil is fat and ugly. Notwithstanding, he fantasises about the possibility of marrying Fraulein Landauer and becoming part of the dynasty.

Sally appears, moody and desperate for a drink. Brian tries to get her to go away, but, while she agrees not to drink, she stays.

Miss Landauer is shown in. Fritz is delighted to see that she is a tall, attractive young woman. Brian cannot get rid of Fritz or Sally. Miss Landauer suggests they have an English speaking 'party'.

Coffee and cakes are brought as they awkwardly speak English. Miss Landauer speaks about a cold, while Fritz enthusiastically tries to ingratiate himself with her, covering his frayed shirt cuffs. He mentions the word 'phlegm', and Brian finds himself in the awkward position of having to explain how it is pronounced. Sally, impudently taking a cue, discusses syphilis, and the scene culminates when she uses the German word for 'screwing', to the horror of all present.

## Scene 16: A park, day

Fritz and Natalia (Landauer), plus Sally and Brian, are riding in the park. Sally is giving Brian her advice for Fritz – that Fritz should just 'lunge' at Natalia.

Later, as Natalia and Sally walk together, Brian asks Fritz how the gigolo business is going. Fritz replies that he thinks he is falling in love with Natalia.

## Scene 17: The Schneider boarding house, night

Sally is preparing to go out to meet her father. She has dressed up, removed her green nail polish, and is very excited. Brian, now showing the publisher his translation, wishes her good luck.

# SUMMARY AND COMMENTARY

### Scene 18: Landauer residence, exterior, night

Brian and Fritz are accompanied to the door by Natalia. Brian thanks her and moves off. Fritz is eloquent, and kisses her, though Natalia is aloof.

Joining Brian at the gate, Fritz expresses wonderment at Natalia's resistance to his charms. Brian advises him, on Sally's behalf, to 'lunge' at Natalia. He is unconvinced.

### Scene 19: Boarding house, night

Sally is sitting in the living room, alone and miserable, when Brian comes in. They move to her room. She tells him that she waited for her father in vain, only to find when she returned a telegram, telling her he could not make the rendezvous. She miserably tells Brian that she's 'nothing'. Seeing how upset she is, Brian comforts her, telling her she is beautiful, talented and a wonderful person. They embrace and kiss. Surprised, she smiles.

### Scene 20: Cabaret, night ('Maybe This Time')

Sally is singing a slow, plaintive ballad, 'Maybe This Time'. The lyrics express the hope that this love affair may at last be the one that works and endures. The scene is intercut with:

### Scene 21: Sally's bedroom, night

Shots of Sally and Brian in bed together in her room, or sitting and smiling at one another across the room. Her singing (at the club) is passionate and poignant.

### Scene 22: Kit Kat Klub, night

Brian enters the club and sees Sally with a fat businessman. He phones her (on the phone system used inside the club). She comes to join Brian, kissing him, and telling him that she got rid of the businessman by telling him she had syphilis. She substitutes for herself the club's transvestite.

### Scene 23: The Landauer house, interior, day

Sally has joined Natalia for afternoon tea. Natalia confesses that she is disturbed. Fritz, whom she did not take seriously, threw himself on her, and the ensuing passion has confused her. They want to marry, but she does not know how to tell her father, since Fritz (she believes) is Christian. Sally suggests she might take him as a lover.

# Commentary

The double love story of this section in the film provides a buoyant and romantic subplot in the middle of the story.

Fritz and Natalia's falling in love is a conventional boy-meets-girl narrative, though it has decidedly comic elements. For a start, Fritz does not intend to fall for her, since he starts from the premise that he only wants her for her money. Then there is the clumsy seduction, along lines suggested by the romantically incompetent Sally, which, against the odds, works. This leaves Natalia in the same situation: being in love and both surprised and embarrassed by it. We enjoy all this, and are almost certainly being invited to have a laugh at the expense of these 'uptight' Germans. Our enjoyment is fairly uncomplicated, and it is difficult to see a deep and meaningful subtext, though Fritz's acceptance of the Jewish Natalia is worth noting.

In the case of Sally and Brian, things are more involved. First as an act of compassion, when Sally is miserable because of her father's indifference, and then in what becomes genuine passion, their love affair develops. Although it gives both obvious pleasure, the film does not overstate the possibilities. In yet another ironic comment on the real life experiences of the principal characters, signalled by constant intercutting, Sally's plaintive love song 'Maybe This Time' tells us of her hopes, but also hints at the possibility that she will be disappointed. We already have a well developed sense of Sally's vulnerability and barely disguised pain (in the matter of her father especially), and know she is exposed emotionally to Brian. Her happiness is very fragile. We should not however be too cynical, nor underestimate the gentle beauty of this period of intimacy between the two friends, who at least for a time are enjoying the pleasures of love. The fledgling love affair is tested in Scene 22, by the 'temptation' of the rich fat man. Sally passes this test with flying colours, rejoining Brian, and affirming our expectation of romance and continuity. However it is a slight test, as we will see.

### Scene 24: Laundry, Berlin, day

Sally enters the laundry, trying to explain in her imperfect German what she wants. She is joined by a handsome young man (Maximilian von Heune), who has picked up something she dropped. He assists her in her explanation. Then he introduces himself, and offers her a ride home. At the door of the laundry, her eyes light up. Across the road is his shining, expensive limousine.

### Scene 25: The Kit Kat Klub, night
### ('Money makes the world go round')

Sally and the MC sing the famous 'Money' song. It is a brilliant and naughty patter song, devoted to the notion that money is the only thing of importance in life.

### Scene 26: Kit Kat Klub, night

An 'Arabian Nights' *tableau vivant* is being performed (naked girls behind a thin cloth, backlit so that their silhouetted bodies are clearly visible). Sally has introduced Maximilian, her new aristocratic friend, to Brian. Brian is sceptical when Sally tells him that she can handle Maximilian. She embraces Brian confidently. At exactly that moment, the MC, watching her, licks his lips lasciviously.

### Scene 27: Sally's bedroom, day

Sally and Brian are in bed asleep, when Maximilian enters, carrying a bottle of champagne and glasses. He thanks her for the previous night and pours a glass for her. She wakes Brian.

## Scene 28: A restaurant, Berlin, day

Brian is waiting alone at the table. Sally appears, showing Brian her beautiful new fur coat. Sally and Maximilian have been on a shopping expedition, and he has been buying her gifts. Brian is wary.

When Sally asks about Brian's present, Maximilian pulls out a gold cigarette case, which he places smilingly on the table. Brian asks why he should accept it, to which Maximilian replies 'to please me'. Sally asks if she can have caviar, and when Maximilian protests that she had caviar for breakfast, she pleads. Laughingly, he tells her she can have caviar whenever she wants.

# Commentary

So far the emphasis has been very much on the relationships – on Sally's desire for love (from her father and from a loyal and fond lover), and Brian's attempts to come to terms with his sexuality.

This sequence in the film introduces a far more cynical notion – that materialism has more importance in people's lives than they would usually like to acknowledge. The cabaret song 'Money' makes this idea particularly plain. Because it is presented in such a comic fashion it is easy to dismiss the idea as a caricature. But in the powerful parallelism which is one of the film's most interesting structural features, we see exactly the same theme taken up in the real life outside the club. When Sally sees the shining limousine, she realises that Maximilian is a 'meal ticket'. His good looks and charm are part of the attraction, but the film not so subtly hints that his wealth is the prime attraction (for example, the cut to the car in Scene 24). This is born out in what then follows – an orgy of self indulgent consumption (furs, caviar, etc). Sally would like to think of herself as a genuine girl, for all her libertarian ways, but deep down she has betrayed herself as being driven by the basest of motives. Brian is at first disdainful of such behaviour and adverse to the consumption which betrays such a shallow attitude, though we must wonder how long he might be able to resist.

### Scene 29: Berlin street, day

Brian and Sally are in Maximilian's limousine. They pass the blanket-covered body of a man. Brian asks about the Nazis (the culprits in this street murder), but Maximilian tells him 'we' (the German people) can handle them and that they are useful as a way of dealing with the Communists. The car drives on into the country.

### Scene 30: Kit Kat Klub, night ('Two Ladies')

The MC's voiceover is heard at the end of the previous scene talking about having two and sometimes even more lovers. The curtains open, revealing him and two women, dressed in German folk costume. The song begins. 'Two Ladies' is a comic song about one man having two mistresses simultaneously. Its high speed caricature of a *menage à trois* (three person relationship) involves choreographed dancing, comic business under a giant bed sheet, and plentiful crotch jokes.

### Scene 31: Maximilian's mansion, day

Maximilian, his butler and a maid lead Brian and Sally upstairs to their rooms. Brian and Sally are obviously overawed at the splendour of the house.

### Scene 32: Sally's bedroom in the mansion, day

Sally is attended by a maid, who lays out sumptuous clothes for her. She is speechless. She looks out the window at the palatial grounds.

### Scene 33: Brian's bedroom in the mansion, day

Maximilian enters and invites Brian to help himself to Maximilian's clothes. He pulls out a sweater and throws it to Brian. Brian asks him about his marriage, and Maximilian tells him he and his wife have an arrangement – living apart, and supporting the arts in their own way. Brian is clearly uneasy about the situation. Maximilian leaves trousers for Brian to wear, and concealed under the folds is the gold cigarette lighter (the gift).

### Scene 34: Dining room, Maximilian's mansion, evening

A dinner party is in progress, all the guests in evening dress. Sally is playing the party girl, boasting about her father and their wonderful relationship. Into this scene is cut a single shot of the MC (at the club) mouthing the word 'money'.

### Scene 35: The lake at Maximilian's estate, day

Sally, Brian and Maximilian are on the lake, Brian rowing them. All are in bathing costume and Maximilian is filming Sally.

### Scene 36: The great hall of Maximilian's house, night

Sally is dancing to the music on the gramophone. Maximilian compliments her. Brian is drinking. Sally invites Maximilian to join her in the dance. Brian looks on, uneasily. He makes a joke about being king of the jungle (a reference to Maximilian's desire to go to Africa and take them with him) but then continues drinking. When Maximilian and Sally go into a slow embrace, Brian watches. Then he joins them, all three of them rotating slowly. We see them looking at one another in an uneasy close up.

The music stops. Brian frees himself and lurches forward. They lay him down on the couch, so drunk that he falls immediately to sleep. Exchanging glances, Maximilian and Sally head off together.

### Scene 37: Maximilian's car, the road back to Berlin, day

As they drive in the limousine back through the countryside from his estate, Maximilian talks about Africa. Sally is asleep. She embraces first Brian, then Maximilian, then stretches out over both men.

### Scene 38: Roadside tavern, countryside, day ('Tomorrow Belongs To Me')

Maximilian and Brian are having a drink in the beer garden of a tavern out in the countryside. The mood is a one of quiet pastoral beauty, expressed in cutaways to horses galloping in the fields, and the benign sunshine. Maximilian admits that he finds Sally tiring, and expresses his relief at her being asleep. He and Brian toast Africa, and look at one another meaningfully.

The music of the band has ceased. A handsome blond boy begins singing a song, 'Tomorrow belongs to me'. At first he sings alone, but soon his song is picked up by a great many of the people in the beer garden. We see that he is wearing a swastika armband, and a number of the audience also are dressed as brown shirts (Hitler's supporters). By the end of the song, there is a patriotic fervour about the singing, as they repeat the lines 'A morning will come when the world is mine,/ Tomorrow belongs to me'.

Brian asks Maximilian if he is still so confident of being able to control the Nazis as they get back into his limousine and drive off. The camera pulls back to a long shot of the whole peaceful country scene, as the rousing end of the song echoes on the soundtrack. The young boy has concluded the song with a Nazi salute.

# Commentary

The beer garden scene is a famous one in *Cabaret*. It was so sensitive that it was cut from the German language edition of the film. German sensitivities were still too great in 1972 to tolerate this blatant reminder that Nazism was not something imposed on the German people from outside, but an expression of their own jingoistic fervour.

The scene is a beautiful example of irony. At first, we are positioned to 'read' the innocent face of the blond boy as an expression of all that is good and pure. Intercut as it is with scenes of horses frolicking and the glorious German countryside, romantic images with connotations of beauty and good, it lulls us into a false sense of uncritical acceptance. The revealed swastika armband is the first sign that all is not as it seems. As the scene goes on and the ordinary country folk in the garden are transformed before our eyes into fervent Nazi sympathisers, we realise with real disquiet that beneath the surface of normality or ordinary life lie these dark capacities for extremes. Significantly one old man does not participate in the standing and joining in. We can surmise that he is Jewish, or that he disagrees with the ideology of the Nazi party. The overall movement however is in favour of the Nazi party. Maximilian's smug assurances now look very doubtful indeed. In contrast, Brian's real concerns are looking more and more appropriate. He effectively comes to express (at least on this point) the unspoken attitudes of the film itself.

### Scene 39: The road outside the Landauer House, day

Natalia comes out the gate and gets into her car. Fritz joins her. She tells him they must never see each other again. As she drives off he calls out, 'Is it the money?' She stops the car. She admits that at first she thought it was, but now she knows him to be honest and true. He asks her to marry him. She tells him it is impossible because she is a Jew and he is not. She drives off, leaving Fritz standing on the road.

### Scene 40: Street outside
### Fraulein Schneider's guest house, day

Maximilian's limousine arrives. Brian gets out. Brian and Maximilian look at one another bleakly without saying a word.

### Scene 41: Sally's room, day

Sally is talking raptuously about going to Africa with Maximilian, and the possibility of being the next baroness. Suddenly she realises what she has said and apologises to Brian. He angrily snaps at her that she should listen to herself, that she is behaving like an underage *femme fatale* [deadly woman]. He adds that she is about as *fatale* as an after dinner mint.

Sally attacks him in return, making snide insinuations about his lack of knowledge of women, and how wonderful (in comparison) Maximilian is. Brian angrily retorts, 'Screw Maximilian!'. Sally says smugly, 'I do.' Brian laughs bitterly and adds, 'So do I.' Sally is appalled. She refers to them as 'you two bastards', to which Brian replies, 'Shouldn't that be three?' Brian goes out and slams the door.

# Commentary

Now the undercurrents involving Brian and Maximilian which were obvious in earlier scenes have become explicit. Brian too has become Maximilian's lover. He has betrayed Sally, just as she has betrayed him. Their love is revealed as a fallible thing, subject to the 'corruption' or temptation posed by the beautiful and wealthy Maximilian. Their loyalty and pretence of devotion is shown to be a sham. While we cannot draw an exact parallel between this subplot and the larger theme of the growing Nazi influence in Germany at that time, there is a sort of echo nonetheless. The apparent innocence and civilised grace of Germany is belied by its capacity for ferocious hatred and violence. In a similar way the apparent civilised charm and goodness of the *menage à trois* (Maximilian, Sally and Brian) is revealed deep down a selfish, grubby and untrustworthy thing. The film is forcing us to confront people's capacity for corruption. It is a theme which unites the personal story and the larger context.

It is worth noting that *Cabaret* is *not* inviting us to disapprove of the homosexuality as such. We must remember that it was made in 1972, before gay rights, and there is an air of uneasiness about the Brian-Maximilian affair, but it is not being set up as a case study in depravity or sin. It is the personal betrayal which offends Sally, not the type of sex. *Cabaret* was considered in its time quite daring to confront a subject which was (in 1972) virtually taboo in mainstream cinema. We should remember that Brian is presented as a highly sympathetic character, and his sexual preferences, while problematical, are not criticised. If the film had been involved in a simple-minded 'gay bashing' mentality, it would not have made Brian and Maximilian so charming, and would have taken care to make its disapproval explicit. (For the record, the original of Brian, Christopher Isherwood himself, was one of this century's most famous homosexuals, and lived much of his life as the partner of another celebrated gay, the playwright and poet W.H. Auden.)

## Scene 42: Berlin street, day

Brian is walking near the railway. He passes a brown shirt handing out leaflets. He takes one and crumples it, telling them their party is crap. They are unmoved, joking about the 'auslander' (foreigner). Then he kicks over a Nazi flag.

### Scene 43: Brian's bedroom, day

Brian is in bed with a blackened eye and bandages. Sally is looking after him. She asks if he took on the whole party, but he says only two people.

She tells him she has something for him. She reads a letter, from Maximilian. He tells them that he has to go to Argentina, and farewells them, saying, 'It was fun'. He has left them 300 marks. Sally bitterly says that means that on an hourly rate they were about the same as a prostitute's rates. Brian and Sally embrace sadly.

# Commentary

A t this point, we should acknowledge that there is a element of assumed 'outside' knowledge built into the film. The setting is 1931, but as seen from the perspective of 1972 (when the film was made) and even later (when it is being studied). We as viewers bring to *Cabaret* a vast amount of information about what Hitler did later (see Background Notes). We cannot help applying this to the film, as the director undoubtedly intended.

Thus, when we contemplate Maximilian, the blond Aryan-style German who has betrayed both his best 'friends', we might well make a parallel between him and the Nazis themselves, who were in the process (at this point in history) of betraying their countrymen and women. Maximilian used Brian and Sally, and then left them. The Nazis used the German people, led them into a disastrous war (and worse, the Holocaust) and then left them to face history and their victims. The Nazis didn't even 'pay off' the German nation. They left it bankrupt and in despair. In Maximilian, the film hints, we have seen something of that colossal arrogance that the Nazis demonstrated: an obscene egotism, and willingness to treat other people as disposable objects. His superficial attractiveness (blond, handsome, wealthy, charming) parallels what for the German people in the 1930s was the attractiveness of the National Socialist Party and its *fuhrer* (devoted to the ideals of perfection, strength, patriotism, etc). In Maximilian's betrayal, however, we are reminded of what was to be in real life the most appalling betrayal of a great and civilised nation.

### Scene 44: Kit Kat Klub, night

A raunchy dance number is in progress, with six women skimpily dressed, wearing black stockings and suspenders. They gyrate around the stage, their dance full of suggestive movements. All at once, one of them is revealed as the MC, dressed like the girls.

At the end of the number, they switch their cloche hats around, instantly converting them to army helmets. Their dance suddenly becomes a goose step, and they march off the stage. The MC, who has taken off his blonde wig, laughs uproariously. This scene is constantly intercut with:

### Scene 45: Garden of the Landauer house, night

Nazi thugs have climbed over the gate, and into the garden. At the front gate they have painted the word 'Juden' (Jews). They chant, 'Juden, Juden', before running off. Natalia comes to the door, and sees the body of her little dog lying dead on the front step.

# Commentary

The rise of Nazism has already emerged as a major theme in *Cabaret*, and these scenes make it even more explicit. Although the dance number (Scene 44) which burlesques Nazi soldiers is presented in a comical way, there is an undercurrent of menace, and the smiles of the MC look quite sinister. The murder of Natalia's little dog and the scrawling of the word 'Juden' are reminders to us of the black racially-inspired madness that was to take over Germany in the years to come. We are never referred (in the movie) to the Holocaust, except by implication. It is a testimony to the stain that has been made on modern history however, that even slight signifiers (like the 'Juden' sign) remind us in a flash of what was to come.

### Scene 46: Library, interior, day

Brian is doing research when Sally appears. He asks her what the matter is. Sally bellows, 'Goddamnit, I'm having a baby!'

### Scene 47: Berlin streets, day

Sally is walking home accompanied by Brian. She tells him she doesn't know whose the baby is. She intends to have an abortion, though it will cost a lot of money.

### Scene 48: The Schneider guest house

Brian and Sally walk down the passage to their doors. Without a word, they unlock their doors and go in. A little time passes, then Brian emerges from his room, crosses the passage and opening Sally's door, says, 'I want to marry you.'

### Scene 49: Sally's room, night

Brian and Sally are surrounded by candles, drinking. They toast themselves and the baby. Sally asks Brian if he minds if it is not his, and he says that he does not. He goes off to his room and comes back smoking his cigar (for the baby). They kiss tenderly.

# Commentary

How are we to take Brian's proposal of marriage? Has he reverted to heterosexuality as a preferred option? No. It is more likely the act of a man who is trying to undo the guilt of his earlier betrayal, to act in an honourable fashion and to act out a compassionate attempt to help. He is perhaps genuinely trying to do what is expected of him. We are invited to see his actions in a sympathetic light, of that there is no doubt at all. But does it mean he has discovered he loves only Sally, and has given up being gay? Hardly. This is one of the most poignant and psychologically subtle aspects of the film, as Brian tries to do 'the right thing', against his own nature. His enactment of the proud father role (right down to the tie and cigar) is funny, but uncomfortable. While perhaps inclined to hope that their relationship will somehow work out, we nonetheless have enough information about both of them by now to wonder if the apparent romance of this episode will prove real or illusory.

## Scene 50: Fraulein Schneider's guest house, interior, day

Brian returns with his bicycle, meeting Fritz in the vestibule. As they pass through the salon, they overhear Herr Ludwig talking about the Jewish conspiracy to take over the world. Brian asks if he believes that, and learns that he read it in a Nazi propaganda paper. Brian jokes disparagingly about a conspiracy of 'horses arses'.

## Scene 51: Brian's room

Fritz is in despair. He declares that Natalia has ruined him, by making him an honest man. Then he tells Brian his secret: he is a Jew. Brian is not put out and suggests that surely if he loves Natalia, this solves his problem. However Fritz tells Brian that now she will throw him out (because he has lied to her) and a Nazi thug will beat him up.

## Scene 52: Kit Kat Klub, night ('If you could see her')

The MC is revealed with a female figure (facing away from the audience and cloaked). He begins to sing a plaintive love song, 'If you could see her through my eyes'. The female figure turns around, revealing a gorilla in a dress. The MC and the gorilla (his pretend girlfriend) go through a whole number dancing and cuddling. He gives her a ring (which he puts in her nose). In mock solemn fashion, he begs the audience for understanding. The song ends with the line, 'If you could see her through her my eyes, she wouldn't look Jewish at all'.

## Scene 53: Landaeur house, exterior, night

Fritz walks up to the front door and bangs on it. He continues banging until the lights come on and the door is opened. He announces simply, 'I am a Jew'.

## Scene 54: The synagogue, day

Fritz and Natalia are being married. Brian and Sally are watching in the congregation. Sally is obviously emotional and joyful, but Brian is looking thoughtful.

# Commentary

Fritz's 'coming out' as a Jew of course bears an important message. Interestingly, nothing of the kind occurs in the original Isherwood stories, underlining the way the filmmakers have introduced a key theme – the issue of authenticity and integrity (see Themes section). Fritz, who has gone through life faking love in return for money (not very admirable), and concealing his true identity (a little more understandable, in the context), now embraces true love and the secret of his Jewishness. He changes from being a fraud to being an authentic and decent person. We do not have to look too hard to see that the movie endorses these qualities. The cinematic qualities of Scene 54, for instance, with its radiant lighting, space and lovely composition, endorses the happy couple and the values (symbolised in the wedding) of honesty and commitment. The scene is especially striking (in its moral decisiveness) in a story which is so morally ambiguous most of the time, and replete with corrupt and amoral individuals. Perhaps the Fritz-Natalia resolution is a little hard to believe, and makes its point a trifle unsubtly, but if we are looking for messages, there *is* one. The affirmation (Scene 54) of the beauty of these two young lovers is yet another subliminal reminder about what was to become (in real history) of people such as them.

## Scene 55: A forest, day

Brian and Sally are picnicking. He is brooding. She is trying to cheer him up. She announces to him that the baby has wonderfully 'solved' all their problems. He makes little attempt to join her sense of good luck and happiness. We cut suddenly to a series of vignettes of earlier moments – Brian drinking with Sally, the three dancing together, Sally dancing and singing, their love, the MC licking his lips.

### Scene 56: The Schneider guest house, night

Sally is coming in sadly. A little boy is sitting on the stairs. She picks up the ball he has dropped and hands it back to him.

### Scene 57: Sally's room, early morning

Brian is asleep in a chair. Sally comes in and lies down on the bed. Brian asks if she did 'it'. She pretends not to understand until he mentions the abortion. She admits it.

He is angry and asks why. Tearfully, she tells him that she is selfish, inconsiderate and has an 'infantile fantasy' about being a great actress. She says that their dreams of living in a little cottage at Cambridge would inevitably have led to them hating one another. She tells him that she really does love him. Brian goes, and Sally lies back on the bed despairingly.

# Commentary

If the Fritz-Natalia ending perhaps strains our credibility, the film returns to psychological realism with its follow up on the Brian-Sally liaison. The same theme of authenticity comes through again.

Sally may be confused and naive, but she is not really a fool. Given a little time, she sees through Brian's valiant but doomed attempt to play the conventional hetero husband. She also, no doubt rightly, anticipates her own discomfort in trying to fulfil the traditional wife and mother stereotype. In opting for the abortion, she is opting for truth. The film does not suggest that abortions are a wonderful thing, or to be entered into lightly (despite Sally's throwaway line about 'one of my whims'), but that they are legitimate in the context of a woman's right to control her own fertility and life (another strikingly modern idea for the time). Sally is hardly ever more sympathetic in the film than in Scene 57, when, heartbroken at the aborted baby and the end of her brief dream of a life with Brian, she confronts reality. The final image is of Sally curled up on the bed – desolate. A high angle shot emphatically reinforces her powerlessness and sense of loss. This is Sally at her most vulnerable.

### Scene 58: Berlin railway station, day

Sally has come to the station to see Brian off (he is returning to England). At the moment of parting, she holds out her hand to shake his. He takes her hand, and smilingly tells her her green nails are shocking. They look at one another, and tears fill her eyes. She goes off, without looking back, but waving her hand at him.

### Scene 59: The Kit Kit Klub, night ('Cabaret')

Sally is offstage, looking melancholy. The MC introduces her. Instantly she puts on her stage smile and goes out to sing 'Cabaret'. The song begins cheerfully, moves through a middle section in which she remembers her dead friend the prostitute Elsie, at which point she seems emotional. Then she moves into the final celebratory moments. We catch the words, 'It isn't that far from cradle to tomb', as the song enjoins us to enjoy life while we can.

### Scene 60: Kit Kat Klub, night

The MC, in a reprise of the first shot, appears out of the mirrored wall surface, telling the audience and viewers, 'Life is beautiful, the girls are beautiful, even the orchestra is beautiful...'. We cut to the orchestra, which plays the *Cabaret* refrain. As they play, and the camera slowly circles, the music fades away. At the end, the MC reappears to say, 'Auf Wiedersehen...[goodbye] A bientôt [see you later]'. At that point he disappears through a curtain at the back of the stage.

The camera pans slowly along the mirrored wall, with a muted drum roll on the sound track. We see the audience reflected, and as the camera comes to a standstill, the stark black of swastikas on arm bands. The frame freezes and the final credits roll.

# Commentary

The departure of Brian is a necessary conclusion to the end of their affair. We should note that while the pretence of a life-long love has been well and truly abandoned, their friendship (love for one another as friends) remains. Not all has been lost. The film is sad but not wholly negative.

The same bitter-sweet idea is picked up in the final song, and the title song, 'Cabaret'. 'What use is sitting alone in your room, come hear the music play...Life is a cabaret old chum, come to the cabaret.' This is the famous and ancient theme of *carpe diem* (live life a day at a time), the idea that while life is full of sadnesses and loss, it also has things in it worth celebrating. 'Come taste the wine, come hear the band...' Let's rejoice while we can.

Nonetheless, as the film ends, in a wonderful mirror image (literally and figuratively) of its beginning, we are reminded for a last time of the darkness. The black swastika armbands are now everywhere in the audience. The Holocaust is coming. Let's not be so committed to a good time that we don't also face up to the truth, and put down the forces that would subvert life and happiness.

# WHAT DOES IT ALL MEAN?
## CHARACTERS, THEMES AND ISSUES

## Characters

### Sally Bowles (Liza Minnelli)

Christopher Isherwood's original Sally (*Goodbye to Berlin*) is a rather tiresome individual. However, the screen Sally is quite different. Thanks to the special charm of Liza Minnelli, and the direction of Bob Fosse, *Cabaret*'s Sally is a beguiling character, flawed but lovable, admirable despite her weaknesses.

Much depends on Minnelli's particular blend of exuberance and vulnerability. She has the throaty voice of her mother (Judy

Garland), and plays the kittenish vamp with real enthusiasm. Yet her wide-eyed girlishness constantly reminds us that to a fair extent, this is all an act, an attempt to 'tough out' a hard world. In her quiet, exposed moments (the tears she weeps when her father abandons her, the poignant song 'Maybe this time'), we see a dreamer and optimist, a good time girl with a heart of gold. Brian recognises that Sally has a fantasy of being a seductress. He even uses the term *femme fatale* (though he says she is *not* one), but the term is not appropriate. She is no 'deadly woman' – but a lost girl playing at seduction. It's true that she is an opportunist, and greedy for fame, who uses people for her own ends, but she is not vicious or evil at heart.

In the film's version of Sally (not the Isherwood), she is the daughter of an American diplomat, who has (to all intents and purposes) cast her off. Homeless, adrift from family and country, she is on a quest for love and glory. Her chronic lack of self-esteem ('Maybe I am just nothing'), her desperate need to prove herself, and join what she sees as the bright world of movies, drive her. She has deliberately acquired a persona, that of the decadent vamp (signalled by the green fingernails, the repeated 'Darling' and the deliberately shocking lifestyle), and uses it as a means of overcoming her basic shyness and sense of inferiority. However, significantly, Brian sees through it. 'You're about as *fatale* as an after dinner mint,' he jokes bitterly. Her earlier attempts at seduction ('Doesn't my body make you wild with desire?') have already betrayed her clumsiness. Deep down, she is no sex goddess, but an ordinary girl who wants love.

By the end of the story, her naive attempts to be a hard-hearted 'gold digger' and tramp have led her to chastening experiences, and she has confronted the truth about herself. The money alone (represented by the tacky affair with Maximilian) is revealed as worthless. Brian's 'love' and long-term commitment to the child (and Sally) was more dutiful than genuine. She knows that it would not work out, no matter what both of them are trying to pretend.

She finally has little more than the consolation of wisdom. Sally has become more responsible for her life. She acknowledges her needs (performance and freedom) and what is *not* for her (conventional domesticity and monogamous commitment). She has gained a sense of bitter-sweet perspective. The last (and title) song, with its confrontation of human imperfection (in Elsie, and herself), and lost dreams, but its celebration of life ('Come taste the wine, come hear the band...'), the joy of the moment, tells us that she understands. Enjoy what you have, for the cabaret (life) will be over before you know it.

## Brian Roberts (Michael York)

A little like Sally, Brian is well-intentioned but naive. At the beginning of the film, he appears the classic 'innocent abroad' – the well brought up, proper English gentleman finding himself in the decadent *demi-monde* of pre-war Berlin. His shock, at Sally's libertarian ways, and the bizarre characters of the club (for example, the transvestite in the toilet), is comical, but also indicative of an 'up tight', narrow-minded quality which needs broadening.

More importantly, he is confused about his own sexual identity. He appears to be a latent homosexual, as evidenced by his embarrassed response to Sally's overtures (Scene 14), but is uneasy with this. His seduction by Sally seems to please him, in that, discovering he can feel desire for a woman, he enjoys a period of going 'straight'. The subsequent seduction, this time by Maximilian, punctures that illusion. He is bisexual, and still confused. We are invited to see the scene in the woods (55) as a hint that Brian knows that marrying Sally, after his impulse proposal (out of pity for her predicament), would undoubtedly be a disaster. The frequent close ups of Brian emphasise his lack of response to Sally's enthusiasm about the baby. Brian is in a dilemma: he has committed himself to a course of action which does not match his real identity. The abortion frees him from this self-imposed trap. They remain good friends, but as lovers the time of romance is finished. Their parting is without illusion. They don't even promise to meet again. It's over, and they know it. Brian has accepted himself for what he is, and will go on (we assume) to his own life, finding his happiness on his own (not straight society's) terms.

In one aspect, however, Brian is neither confused nor a doubtful figure. An important thematic strand of the film is picked up in his strong aversion to the Nazis. This is made very clear in both his lack of prejudice (when Fritz tells him that he's Jewish, Brian is immediately accepting, in stark contrast to the Germans we see) and in his active confrontation with the brown shirts. He rejects (implicitly) Maximilian's facile dismissal of them, and takes them on. He ends up bruised and sore for his efforts, but at least he has stood up for his principles.

Alone in the film, he is the one who speaks out against the coming menace, and it goes without saying that we are positioned to see him as right.

### Maximilian von Heune (Helmut Griem)

At first, we are invited to read Maximilian as the ideal man. He is blond, handsome, wealthy and charming. He is certainly what Sally thinks she wants (for a time). He is the epitome of European civilisation itself – urbane and sophisticated. He 'seduces' us as much as he does Sally and Brian. He is, we might almost say, an 'Aryan' ideal. Certainly, if Hitler could have visualised the perfect German, Maximilian might have been that person. Like the boy singing in the beer garden, he is a teutonic stereotype – of the blond, blue-eyed *ubermensch* (master race).

That this all turns out to be an illusion is the whole point. Maximilian is a user. He consumes people the way he drinks champagne. They are useful to him for his pleasure. They are disposable at will, when he is tired of them. His 'love' affair with both Sally and Brian is as genuine as his tease about the African trip. Maximilian finally abandons them, and pays them off, leaving them understanding that he has used them as he would a prostitute. Maximilian is a much more subtle version of the theme which, in its fully fledged version, we can identify with the Nazis (to whom he is implicitly compared by the film). This works initially through visual similarities between Maximilian and the young boy (both blond, blue-eyed and handsome). By implication, both characters can be read as exemplars of the dangerous excesses beneath the ostensible glory of Nazi Germany. He is an embodiment of the idea that the strong (or in his case, wealthy and clever) take what they want. Morality is irrelevant. Appetite rules. Maximilian would be far too discreet an exploiter to beat people up, or send them to gas chambers. He merely consumes them, and pays them off. He is quite simply amoral.

His is real decadence, which goes far beyond sexual

irregularities, into the darker realm of an loveless indifference. In contrast to both Sally and Brian, who, for all their weaknesses, do have loyalty, fondness and good intentions on their side, Maximilian is essentially cold-hearted and lacking compassion. Like other aspects of life (as depicted in the film), appearances are deceiving. Corruption comes in all forms, many of them dangerously attractive on the surface.

### The Master of Ceremonies (Joel Grey)

The MC is never named, and that suits the concept well, for he is not a 'rounded' character at all. He is part caricature, part symbol. He embodies to a great extent the tawdry world of the cabaret, and beyond it, symbolically, the quagmire of Weimar Germany as it slid towards the Nazi era.

'Decadence' finds its comic, theatrical face in the MC. He invites us to have a good time. 'Here, everything is bewdiful,' he purrs, painting the cabaret as a kind of paradise. Enjoy. Consume whatever you like. Don't feel guilty, just do it. He tempts us to enjoy pornography ('It's a battle to keep their clothes on...Who knows, to-night we might lose the battle...'), mud wrestling, materialism ('Money makes the world go round'), promiscuity ('Two ladies'), cross-dressing – and, as the tone turns darker, racial vilification ('If you could see her through my eyes, she wouldn't look Jewish at all.') and militarism (as in the goose-stepping dance).

Like the cabaret itself, he suggests that all is in fun. Yet there is an ironic (contradictory) subtext to the character, as there is to the cabaret. As signified by his rouged lips, yellow teeth, his smiles (which, in close up, are leers), his gender ambiguity, his knowing smirks – we see that the impression of fun and carefree happiness is a sham. Through the camerawork (extreme close ups and shots of Joel Grey's eyes and mouth) we see that he is toying with the viewer. He is a vaguely diabolical character, who seems to invite us to slide into a pit of self-indulgence. His implied philosophy is, 'Who cares? Anything goes'. It is a theme that looks more and more dangerous as the film goes on.

By the end, as the seedy MC farewells us in his cold way, and the camera pans to the Nazis in the audience, the thematic connection is well established. Amoral self-indulgence, for all its superficial charm, has the capacity to subvert whole societies and overthrow the balance of the world.

# Themes
## 'Life is a cabaret' – the *carpe diem* theme

*C*abaret is entertaining, but underlying its story is a considerable sadness. There is a tension here. If this were a traditional Hollywood musical, we might expect only good times and a utopian cheer. The film presents us with dysfunctional characters (not the stereotypic ideal men and women of movies like *The Sound of Music*), and a decidedly downbeat personal narrative (at least in Sally and Brian's case).

One theme acts as a bridge between the melancholy (of Sally's dysfunctional life, the abortion, etc) and the *joie de vivre* to which she aspires and which the cabaret more or less successfully represents. It is the idea of *carpe diem* (live for the day).

> What good is sitting alone in your room?
> Come hear the music play.
> Life is a cabaret old chum,
> Come to the cabaret.
> Come taste the wine,
> Come hear the band...

This is the notion that life is finite, and often sad, but let's find pleasure in it where we can. We might be tempted to dismiss this theme as a glib cliché, but it is an ancient one, found across a range of texts, and if there is any overall summative comment that can be taken from the film, this might be it.

Sally has a heart of gold, but faulty judgement in men and lifestyle. She means well, but her love life is a disaster and her dreams of the bright lights look like remaining just a fantasy. What's left? Her optimism, her enthusiasm about people, her determination to enjoy whatever happens. What seems at first glance silly affectations – her addiction to the word 'Darling', her eagerness to shock and play the vamp – come after a while to seem more part of her determination to keep her chin up, no matter what. Her father may not love her, but what the heck, let's have fun. Her men may use and leave her, but there's another song to sing, another audience to love her, and who knows, 'Maybe this time...'. Life is short, 'It's only a step from cradle to tomb', she sings, so let's have fun while it lasts.

It is possible to interpret this as a somewhat desperate, and possibly amoral, philosophy, but there is also something appealing about it. Even if the smile she puts on in the last song is a little forced (she's been dumped by two men, lost a baby, has no movie career, and only an endless succession of identical cabaret numbers to look forward to), it expresses something eternally hopeful to which we respond. The choice of Liza Minnelli for the Sally role was inspired, because her style of acting and performing conveys exactly the right sort of fragile happiness to match this idea. She personifies the good time girl who knows that 'the show must go on'. Find that smile and persevere. That's what life is all about.

## Moral integrity and the search for authenticity

*Cabaret* is not a profound film, as at least one critic has reminded us. It is cheeky and entertaining. It doesn't take itself too seriously. But underpinning its exploration of the lives of its principal characters is at least one completely serious idea: that life is best lived by some sort of standard, if only the traditional notion of integrity, or as Shakespeare put it, 'To thine self be true.' How is this theme expressed?

For Brian, it's two issues. Most obviously, there is his rejection of the Nazis. It would have been easy (we may speculate), for a foreigner (and an Aryan-looking man at that) to take no notice of the Nazi threat. So what that they are 'horse's arses', talking arrant nonsense? He could say nothing. He doesn't. He stands up for the truth (about the so-called Jewish conspiracy) and for decency. He gets himself beaten up for his trouble. But there is no regretting the action, which was a form of affirmation of morality.

More subtly, there is the matter of his sexual identity. He flirts for a while with the possibility of heterosexual orthodoxy and parenting. He has an affair with Sally and tries on the role of the straight lover. He proposes marriage to her. But it is clearly a battle. We may admire his motives (especially in seeking to 'rescue' Sally from her predicament), but we see that he is trying too hard to be what he is not. The abortion, and Sally's honesty, releases him from his commitment, and he ends the affair. However unfashionable an ending it was (especially for 1972), it expresses again the idea of being true to yourself, not doing what everyone else expects. The film's refusal to twist the Sally-Brian liaison into a 'happily ever after' ending is quite radical, and argues something important: confront the truth (however uncomfortable), and live with it.

For Sally, though her pretences distract us a little more, something similar is going on. She has the abortion because she knows it wouldn't work out with Brian. She weeps over her father's indifference, but then gets on with her life. She farewells Brian, because their love affair was not meant to last. In the final analysis, Sally is not a 'tramp', or a faker, but a sincere person.

Fritz too confronts the truth. He is at first a male 'whore' (literally). He fakes love in return for money. His charm cannot disguise the amoral nature of his life. Yet he too is redeemed. His acceptance of his Jewishness is a kind of 'coming out' (like Brian's implied acceptance of his homosexuality), and it is all the more admirable given the perilous context in which it takes place (Nazi Germany).

These characters, who deserve our admiration because of what they are, stand in stark contrast to people like Maximilian (for whom life is a hedonistic indulgence) and the characters glimpsed at the cabaret (where anything goes, and you can pretend to be whatever you like). We must not overstate this theme, which is presented with some delicacy, but it does underpin the film. If *Cabaret* at times seems to be celebrating decadence, we should consider how it positions us to read Maximilian and the MC (the truly decadent characters). Sally's heart of gold, Brian's honesty, Fritz's moment of self-affirmation, are the real touchstones of good in a film that flirts with immorality and depravity. It is rather more sceptical (about wickedness) and old-fashioned than we might think.

## Identity and illusion

*Cabaret* begins and ends with a distorting mirror. This is an apt metaphor in a film which so often plays with illusion and the unstable nature of identity (or appearance), both inside the Kit Kat

Klub, and in the wider world outside.

Sally thinks she is a sophisticated woman of the world, priding herself on her green fingernails, which she sports as a sign of 'divine decadence'. She is revealed by the events of the film to be instead something of a damaged person, whose yearning for the silver screen is quickly eclipsed by her wish to be a wife and mother, given the chance. Brian puts his finger on the delusion when he tells her she's 'about as *fatale* as an after dinner mint'. Brian tries for a time to be a regular heterosexual guy, to the point of embarking on a would-be marriage to Sally. She, fortunately, sees through the pretence, and he is able (we assume) to resume his real identity as a gay man (with bisexual leanings). Fritz pretends to be a good Aryan, disguising his Jewishness until love forces it out. Maximilian appears to be the perfect man, until his 'corruption' of Sally and Brian shows him to be a callous user.

The film seems to be implying that identity is not fixed, but malleable, fluid, maybe even arbitrary. The theme of transformation is picked up in the 'real world' setting of the film – as in the conversion of the German people from peaceful folk into fascistic zealots (in the beer garden scene). It certainly suggests that appearance and reality can be very different. This idea is represented in comic form in the cabaret sequences, where switches of identity and illusion are commonplace. The MC turns into a woman, and back again. The 'object of love' turns out to be a gorilla, but the last line of the song changes this to Jew. The chorus girls turn into soldiers, goose-stepping off the stage. The 'bewdiful' orchestra, close up, look like tired old has-beens. Theatre of course is a world of illusion, of make-believe and identity switching. *Cabaret* hints that this is what happens in the real world too.

## The Nazi threat

While *Cabaret* stops short of showing us what happened to the Jews during the so-called 'Final Solution' (see Background Notes), perhaps largely because its setting is 1931 (and the worst excesses of the Holocaust were still almost a decade away), it tells us enough to act as a salutary reminder of that barbarous episode in modern history.

The Nazi threat is depicted in three obvious case studies, and in a good deal of background information. The primary narratives are: what happens to the Kit Kat Klub owner (murdered by Nazi thugs outside his own establishment); the harassment of Natalia (the word 'Juden' scrawled at her gate, and her pet dog murdered); and the confrontation between Brian and the brown shirts (who beat him up). At regular intervals there are references in the club to the Nazi phenomenon: the swastikas in the audience, the Jewish allusions (for example, 'If only you could see her through my eyes'), the goose-stepping dance. Also throughout the film, there are background references. As Brian and Sally walk along the streets of Berlin, we catch glimpses of posters defaced. The people in Fraulein Schneider's guesthouse make racist comments about Jews. We see a dead body in the street. In the beer garden scene, the Aryan youth sings the Nazi anthem, 'Tomorrow belongs to me'. The final shot ends on a freeze frame of the audience, with swastikas everywhere in evidence, a sign of the coming horror.

How are we positioned? The film takes a strongly anti-Nazi line. The Nazi elements constantly intrude into the main narratives (by means of dramatic cross-cutting), keeping the theme before our eyes, at least as a background issue. The beating of the nightclub owner is bestial and disgusting. The killing of the dog is despicable. Even the beer garden scene is a set piece in slowly revealed nastiness. For instance, the camera starts on the youth's face, an angelic one, and then tilts down to reveal the armband, a shock calculated to underline the all-pervasive danger of the regime, and supported in the rest of the scene by the increasingly emotional fervour of the patrons.

It is neither original nor difficult to disapprove of the Nazis. But that the film chooses to tackle this serious issue in what could have been an entirely frivolous entertainment, speaks once again of its radical (for a musical) and serious stance.

## The temptation of 'decadence'

The concept of 'decadence' is central to any discussion of *Cabaret*. It is evoked by the seedy atmosphere of the Kit Kat Klub, with its self-consciously tacky performers and oddball patrons. It is specifically mentioned as early as Scene 4. Sally *wants* to be decadent, the club *is* decadent, and many of the characters and events of the main narratives *seem* decadent. Yet the film is ambivalent, even contradictory, in its representations and evaluation of 'decadence'. It seems to be have two stances on the concept. It accepts the usefulness of play, performance, even narcissism. Although what Sally calls 'divine decadence' is characterised as self-indulgent, it is not judged harshly, because its consequences are harmless. However, the film also argues that there is also a much more dangerous form of decadence, which *can* lead to harm, if not evil. In Sally and Brian, the film's sympathetic leads, we see the idea that everyone has a price, that people 'sell' themselves out. It is to their credit however that *they* get beyond this self-prostitution (Brian by his stand against the Nazis, Sally in the matter of the baby and Brian), but others, the film implies, just sink deeper into the morass.

For Sally, the concept (her 'divine decadence') seems to be equated with freedom (from old-fashioned, puritanical restraint), variety and play. Thus the green fingernails are her sign of 'decadence', though to us they are a relatively innocent adornment, symbolising little more than cosmetic rebelliousness. Likewise, her screaming as the train goes by seems harmless extravagance. Even when she moves into the area of sexual promiscuity, her essential innocence and goodness of heart prevent us from condemning her too harshly. Indeed, far from throwing away all morality and self-restraint (a possible definition of 'decadence'), the decisions Sally makes towards the end (not to have the child, and to give up Brian), affirm in her an honesty and integrity, actions which place her outside the parameters of 'real' decadence.

The film argues that there is a far more disturbing form of decadence than Sally's naive charade of being corrupt. *Cabaret* slowly builds up a catalogue of decadent acts in a number of settings, locations and narratives: the mudwrestling, the gigolo and prostitute references, the Nazi violence and anti-Semitism, Maximilian's cold-blooded campaign to 'corrupt' Sally and Brian. We are able to see that Sally is flirting with a dissolution of values that, allowed to run unchecked, *can* end up 'decay' or depravity.

The film does not explore the complexities of this issue, for that is not part of its discourse. It leaves us, the viewers, to speculate afterwards. A certain amount of licence is healthy, it seems to imply. Don't be too 'bourgeois', too narrow-minded and judgemental. Freedom is everyone's right. The 'camp' or carnival qualities of the cabaret are the stylistic expression of this theme. However, beyond freedom lie the dangers of anarchy, nihilism (a belief in nothing at all), the unrestrained gratification of whatever instincts rise to the surface – lust, hatred, exploitation, a hunger for power, and finally an unfettered amorality (a life without any concept of morals). These, the film hints, are truly disturbing. Personified as they are – theatrically in the figure of the MC (whose diabolic mock smiles suggest a timeless amorality), socially in the seductive but finally repugnant figure of Maximilian, and politically in the ravages of the Nazis – they *are* 'decadence' – the dissolution of all values, the loss of all safeguards – and, *Cabaret* argues, this form of decadence is a *real* threat to society.

## Sexual diversity and the argument for tolerance

*Cabaret* was an early favourite in the gay movement, insofar as it is a movie which advocates gay rights, whether overtly or by implication. A clearer example is *The Rocky Horror Picture Show* (1975), with its wildly 'camp' style, cross-dressing and deliberate flaunting of sexual orthodoxy. *Cabaret* is far more subtle, but it does embrace sexual differences, and in its representation of a sympathetic gay protagonist, argues for tolerance and inclusiveness.

*Cabaret* was not the first movie to show homosexuality, it goes without saying. There had been innuendo and naughtiness aplenty, when for example Marlene Dietrich dressed as a man, or Kenneth Williams played the camp clown in the *Carry On* series. Hollywood had long made comic fun out of cross-dressing, as for example in the Marilyn Monroe classic *Some Like it Hot* (where Tony Curtis and Jack Lemmon disguise themselves as women in an all-girl orchestra), and continues to do so. But serious treatments of being gay were rare, at least in mainstream movies.

In 1969, *Midnight Cowboy* came out, a story in which the poor boy from the country (Jon Voight) comes to New York to find fame, and ends up instead a male prostitute. It won an academy award. The same year, the film adaptation of D.H. Lawrence's classic novel

*Women in Love* appeared, with its famous nude wrestling scene (two men), though the homosexual subtext was never acknowledged. In 1971, the well-known play *The Boys in the Band* (about homosexual partners) came to the screen. In 1971, Visconti's *Death in Venice* brought to the screen Thomas Mann's famous novella about a great man who becomes obsessed with a beautiful boy. *Sunday Bloody Sunday* (1971) was another early attempt to 'normalise' gay relations. But the movies' treatment of the issue continued to be problematical. Where *Midnight Cowboy*, *Sunday Bloody Sunday* and *Death in Venice* had been sympathetic, even celebratory, other films indulged in what amounted to 'gay bashing'. Fellini's *Satyricon* (about ancient Rome, 1971) showed homosexual relations as part of its portrayal of Roman debauchery, while in *Deliverance* (1972), it is the villains who rape one of the male characters. In *Tommy* (1975), it is the depraved paedophile uncle who abuses the title character. Pornographic films, such as the famous *Emmanuelle* series (1974-) began to routinely depict lesbian relations, but as part of a voyeuristic ritual for male heterosexual consumption, not as a genuine way of exploring lesbian issues.

*Cabaret* anticipates the gay rights movement by some years, and is part of that broad-based attempt to have 'straight' society accept the right of gay people to live, and love, their own way. The film's exploration of sexual diversity is quite radical, for the time. If we count the variations in the film, we note a wide range: heterosexual relations (Fritz-Natalia, and Brian-Sally), homosexual (Maximilian-Brian), bisexual (Brian), transvestism (the man in drag in the toilet), lesbianism (the ladies at Fraulein Schneider's), pornography (Herr Ludwig's publishing and the nude *tableau vivant*) and cross-dressing (the MC), not to mention prostitution (male and female). These are all presented as part of the libertarian world of pre-war Berlin, and we readily accept them in such an exotic context.

It is in its depiction of Brian, however, that the film makes its most daring and serious attempt to mould the audience's attitudes. His is one of the very earliest screen cases of what is now called 'coming out', and together with a very small number of quality films of that period (mentioned above), in the vanguard of what was to be a major social movement.

# WHAT THE CRITICS SAY

It's difficult to make any movie – the script, the egos, the weather, all contribute to submarining a production. The audience never sees any of that and can only concern itself with the result. So when a great movie comes along, it's a miracle. *Cabaret* was one of those rare stage musicals that became even better on the screen. Using the Kit-Kat Klub, a seedy, smoky *boite* [nightclub], as the central location, Fosse and Allen provide a film that throbs with passion. Minnelli is an American singer in 1930s Berlin who falls in love with York, a mild-mannered writer who manages to mature in the course of the action. They are both seduced by Helmut Griem, a wealthy playboy suffering from Cole Porter's 'old ennui' [boredom with the world]. Marisa Berenson is the Jewish heiress to a department store fortune and she falls in love with Fritz Wendel, who also is Jewish but has been keeping that a secret as the National Socialist party begins to emerge. Minnelli gets pregnant, York confronts his bisexuality, and all five characters interact with the scenes at the Kit Kat Klub. Joel Grey (who won a supporting actor Oscar) is the MC at the club and the only other major player (besides Minnelli) who sings in the movie. This is more a drama with music than your old-fashioned musical. Kander and Ebb wisely tossed out several of their weaker efforts from the score of the play and added much better songs for the film. Fosse has managed to keep an underlying feeling of danger; no matter how happy the songs and dances, you can't help feeling that there's a Nazi lurking in the wings, ready to bring his club down on any one of his characters...Although it seems fashionable these days to denigrate *Cabaret*, it was explosive when it burst on the 1972 scene and deservedly won Oscars [for Minnelli and the crew]. (Jay Robert Nash & Stanley Ralph Ross, *The Motion Picture Guide*, 1927-1983, Cinebooks Inc, Chicago, 1985)

The film version of (the 1966 John Kander-Fred Ebb Broadway musical) *Cabaret* is most unusual: it is literate, bawdy, sophisticated, sensual, cynical, heart-warming, and disturbingly thought-provoking. Liza Minnelli heads a strong cast. Bob Fosse's generally excellent direction recreates the milieu of Germany some 40 years ago...The screenplay, which never seems to talk down to an audience, while at the same time making its candid points with tasteful emphasis, returns the story to a variety of settings. The sleazy cabaret remains a major recurring set.

The choice of Minnelli for the part of Sally Bowles was indeed daring. Good-hearted quasi-sophisticated amorality and hedonism are not precisely Minnelli's professional bag, and within many scenes she seems to caroom from golly-gee-whiz-down-home rusticity to something closer to the mark. (Derek Elley, *Variety Movie Guide*, Prentice Hall General Reference, New York, 1992)

In only her fourth feature, Liza Minnelli lights up the screen as the wild and electrifying Sally Bowles in Bob Fosse's *Cabaret*, which was shown last night before an invited audience that included the cast and director. The role was clearly tailored to suit Liza's exuberant style and warm, throaty voice, reminiscent of her mother – Judy Garland. The brashness that covers the insecurities of her character is perfectly suited to the brashness that covered the insecurities of Berlin in the 30s. Of course she is too good a singer to be found in such a sleazy dive as the Kit Kat Klub, but who cares? Her songs are put over with such bite and passion, and her acting carries a moving conviction. Sally Bowles, an American stranded in Germany on the eve of Europe's cataclysm, is not as decadent as she thinks she is and indeed, in her scenes with Michael York, the young, innocent Englishman abroad, she is both vulnerable and lovable. Bob Fosse has wisely jettisoned most of the stage musical, but has kept the cabaret itself at the centre of the movie. With excellent colour pho-tography and editing, the nightclub is seen to reflect the frenetic and ugly nature of German society at that time, with the brilliantly clever songs providing a pungent commentary on the situation. Joel Grey's lewd, sexually ambivalent and anti-Semitic MC provides the right tone throughout. (*Chronicle of the Cinema*, London-Dorling Kindersley, 1995)

*Cabaret* owes more to the original *Berlin Stories* of Christopher Isherwood and to John Van Druten's play *I Am a Camera* than to the recent Broadway musical of the same name. It is, according to a knowl-edgeable German acquaintance, a fairly accurate recapturing by

Director Bob Fosse of the mood and atmosphere of Berlin of the early 30s. The decadence of Sally Bowles (Liza Minnelli) and her world is portrayed together with the rise of Nazism.

The film is primarily a vehicle for Miss Minnelli...a sad-faced, open-mouthed, wide-eyed conception of insecurity and desperation...Playing the Christopher Isherwood character (on Broadway, an American writer; here, a British language student), Michael York relies too heavily on mannerisms. Happily, Joel Grey is on hand to recreate his award-winning tour de force stage performance as the Master of Ceremonies – an Archie Rice of Berlin. His eyes are narrowed to a venal stare and his mouth frozen to a permanent leer, as he sings his role, escape from the horror of the real world....

...*Cabaret* may make a star out of Miss Minnelli, but it will be remembered as a chilling mosaic of another era's frightening lifestyle. (Alvin H Marill, *Films In Review*, March 1972, Vol 23, No 3)

The breakthrough musical of [the modern type] was *Cabaret*, and though it is still too early to know whether or not it is a freak, its quality and success may establish it in movie history as a pivotal work.

*Cabaret*, in the first place, is tough, stinging, satirical, and acid. None of the sweetness of Rodgers and Hammerstein here; none of the wholesome goodness of *The Sound of Music* in which life is depicted with utter falsity as one big happy songfest. *Cabaret* owes more to the Weill-Brecht spirit of *The Threepenny Opera*, an uncompromising, hard-nosed look at life consistent with the coming of age of America in the 1960s...

*Cabaret* uses music in an exciting new way. Characters do not burst into song to express their emotions. Rather, a sleazy night club called the Kit Kat becomes a place where satirical comment on the lives and problems of these characters is made in striking, entertaining, and often savage dances and songs. Unlike a street in Spanish Harlem or a meadow in the Austrian Alps, the Kit Kat Klub is a logical place for music, and yet the entwining of the music performed in the cabaret and the story of Sally Bowles and her friends is as unnatural as the drama-music mix in any musical. The difference is that the fantasy in *Cabaret* is not disguised by the pseudonaturalism of the integrated musical. It is clearly artificial and no attempt is made to have it any other way.

Moreover, like all great musicals, *Cabaret* is 'right'. Liza Minnelli (daughter of Judy Garland and Vincente Minnelli) is the catalyst. She enlivens the story by her gifts for dramatic acting, and becomes bigger than life when belting out songs on the Kit Kat Klub stage. She is the force that unifies the sly, cruel satire of Joel Grey (the cabaret's MC and the personification of a decadence beyond good and evil), the superbly stylized art direction inspired by German expressionist painting, the handsome and intricate camerawork, and the choreography and dramatic direction of Bob Fosse. *Cabaret* is not unforgettable, it is not profound, it is not great art, but it is great entertainment, a daring piece of diverting escapism that hopefully will revitalize a tired form. (William Bayer, *The Great Movies*, Ridge Press, London, 1973)

Hal Prince's 1966 Broadway production of *Cabaret* was arguably the single greatest achievement of the post-war musical theatre...a musical masterpiece full of guts and daring and incomparable brilliance. Bob Fosse's 1972 cinematic version of the musical play is no less of a triumph...

The Kit Kat Klub remains the centre of the action, only more so, the funhouse that distorts and grotesques reality and as such illuminates it all the more clearly. The songs, the sketches, the dieosities of the freakish nightclub entertainments run parallel in a desperate downhill run with the main story line and the surrounding rise of Nazism in Germany, and the action is swiftly and deftly intercut between the three-as-one like a deformed holy trinity.

In this intertwining, Fosse shows his hand most brilliantly. Not only in the focusing of the nightclub numbers – the songs and their stagings are a perfection of horror and wit in themselves and by their very nature theatrical, so that confining them all to the physical stage is the obvious and logical thing to do – but in the way the numbers on the inside point up and just slightly underline what's going on the outside. Nothing is superfluous, and everything dovetails with ease, and more importantly, with enormous subtlety. While the white face, black knickered whores are knocking the audience over the head with vulgarity, Fosse insidiously slips in the Fascists knocking Germany over the head with something called National Socialism. Where it would have been easy and almost excusable to be heavily obvious, Fosse pulls back just in time and often before, until one is really, convincingly hooked and wanting more. I don't recall seeing any physically ugly Nazis – they're all calm, blond giants on the surface and in daylight – but we do see the after effects of their presence, and that's not quite so pleasant.

This undershocking – and thus shattering – technique culminates in the highpoint of the film, the beer garden song 'Tomorrow Belongs to Me', and never before has the almost irresistible attraction of Nazism and its equally irresistible rise been more clearly, simply, and beautifully put across. In terms of cinematic revelation and story telling, it can only be compared with the ape sequences in Kubrick's *2001*. Spine chillingly simple and absolutely perfect, it is one of the great moments in cinema...Equally magnificent is the look of *Cabaret*. Seldom has colour and design been used to such great effect in re-creating a period feel – perhaps in a few Continental films, especially Italian ones, but never before in any American/ English period films – and photographed with such directness and precision. Again insidious subtlety creeps in as a coverall summation. While it is a major landmark in the musical cinema, and while it may not be perfect, it's as close as we're likely to come in a long, long time. (Peter Buckley, *Films & Filming*, July 1972, Vol 18, No 10)

# SAMPLE ESSAY

'For all its show of fun and careless self-indulgence, *Cabaret* confronts some dark and serious issues.'

Discuss.

*From the opening scene, in which the Master of Ceremonies invites the audience to believe that 'here, life is beautiful', to the final song, with Sally singing 'Life is a cabaret', <u>Cabaret</u> creates an aura of cheerful abandon. This may be Berlin in 1931, but the show must go on. Musical dramas generally set out to entertain, and <u>Cabaret</u> is no exception. For all their tacky air of 'decadence', the Kit Kat numbers are unfailingly fun, and our identification with good time girl Sally encourages us to be optimistic, if not to relish her self-indulgence. But behind the glitzy carnival atmosphere of the club lies a darker truth. And in the lives of Sally and Brian all is not well. The film cleverly balances entertainment and insight. It is celebrated for its musical charms, but also for its quite serious ideas.*

*The Kit Kat Klub strives for the illusion that everything within its walls is harmless play. The MC invites the audience to let go their inhibitions and enjoy the show. And he succeeds. The song and dance acts which are the film's main link are faultless technically. Bob Fosse's celebrated choreography, and his flair as a stage director, work their magic. Liza Minnelli's Sally is superb as the show's talented, luminous star.*

*Offstage, Sally tries to continue the glitzy, everything-is-wonderful act. Sporting green fingernails, delighting in her 'divine decadence', cheerfully promiscuous and flamboyant, she seems to be sailing through life as if it were a set of thrills to be enjoyed while the opportunity remains. She flirts, screams, falls in and out of love (with Brian and Maximilian), drinks, indulges for a time in the luxury of wealth (Maximilian), and despite an abortion bounces on with her life, declaring that 'Life is a cabaret, old chum, come to the cabaret'.*

*A superficial viewing of the film suggests that it is devoted to a brilliant theatrical spectacle, with a little human interest on the side.The truth is more complicated. From the very outset, we have been getting hints about another dimension. The leering MC, with his bright red lips and yellow teeth, the 'orchestra' in suspender belts, the grotesques both in the cast and the audience, are the first clues to a darker reality. Later, it crystalises in the smirking amorality of the Money song, the cross-dressing, the goose-stepping dance and the gorilla song (a racist taunt at the Jews). Inside the club, drunken Nazis are laughing at the women mud wrestlers. Outside, brownshirts are beating to death the owner of the club in an alley. In the street, a body lies after a Nazi bashing. This all culminates in the beer garden scene. A handsome Aryan youth begins to sing 'Tomorrow belongs to me'. The audience join in. Then we see the swastika on his arm, and realise that the song is a Nazi anthem.*

*The Nazis and their victims are not the only serious theme picked up by <u>Cabaret</u>. Brian is trying to come to terms with his sexuality. He allows himself to fall in love with Sally, swept up by her gaiety and vulnerability. Then Maximilian comes along, bent on 'corrupting' them both. He succeeds. Sally's simple-minded 'gold digger' mentality is exposed for what it is. And Brian's bisexuality cannot resist the temptation of the handsome Maximilian. Sally's brief dream of a life with Brian comes up against the reality of his sexual preferences, and her nature. At least they have the courage to be themselves, and face the truth. They part, as friends, have recognised one another for what they are, without illusion.*

*For all its theatrical charm, and its very real beauty as a film, <u>Cabaret</u> asks us to confront some serious ideas. Unlike the heroines of other musicals, Sally doesn't get the guy at the end. Her life remains empty, her despair held off only by the stage ('Life is a cabaret'). In Brian, we see a gay man forced to confront his nature, and accept what he is. In the Nazis, we see the coming Holocaust, and glimpse their victims. Overall, the film reminds us that appearance and reality are different things. The mirror that begins and ends the film is symbolic. Life is complex, and there are no easy answers. <u>Cabaret</u> is fun, but it is anything but foolish. It is no happily-ever-after Hollywood crowdpleaser. It makes us think, and urges us to confront quite serious issues.*

# ESSAY TOPICS

'Both Sally and Brian are forced to confront their true nature, and become better people for it.'

Do you agree?

'Life is a cabaret...' sings Sally Bowles in the final song.

How does the film use the cabaret as a metaphor for life?

Sally likes to think of her lifestyle as 'divine decadence'.

How decadent is she, and the people around her?

'*Cabaret* is highly entertaining, but it has a serious message.'

Discuss.

'Sally and Brian and tempted, and give way, but they are also redeemed by their own acts of courage and honesty.'

Discuss.

'*Cabaret* is a radical film in both its style and its politics.'

Do you agree?